W9-AOK-444

Here, in Eddie Kantar's unique, humorous style, is a truly new bridge experience: the chance to try your hand at playing *and* defending the same contracts! Fifty hands to play, and virtually the same fifty to defend, selected with the author's acclaimed expertise and teaching skill. When you meet hands like these at the table, you'll be ready to make *or* defeat the contract...and you'll smile—or laugh out loud—as you learn!

"Best value in a bridge book that we have seen for quite a while." —Charles Goren and Omar Sharif, GOREN BRIDGE

"If you own a reliable crystal ball, you may not need ...this fine, new book." —Alfred Sheinwold, SHEINWOLD ON BRIDGE

"An excellent book which I recommend to all players." —Bobby Wolff, THE ACES ON BRIDGE

* Selected as Book of the Year by the American Bridge Teachers Association!

A New Approach To
PLAY AND DEFENSE
Volume 1

100 New Problems – in Matched Pairs
– To Play Both Ways

Edwin B. Kantar

Griffin Publishing
Glendale, California

10   9   8

IBSN: 1-882180-07-0

Griffin Publishing
544 West Colorado Street
Glendale, California

Manufactured in the United States of America.

FOREWORD

This book is a little different from the last four quiz books I have written—"Test Your Play" Volumes I and II and "Kantar for the Defense" Volumes I and II.

"A New Approach to Play and Defense" still features 100 problems with "Key Lesson Pointers" to reinforce the thrust of the hand. The themes of each problem are still listed in the Appendix so that you can check your rare error to see if there is a common denominator. The problems are still aimed at intermediate-advanced players who would like their peers to respect their game.

As usual there are a few insulting problems (too easy for you), along with a few toughies (too hard for your partner). The bidding still follows standard lines; 15–17 one notrump range; weak twos; five card majors in first or second seat, but don't die of shock if the opener has AKQx, weak jump overcalls; etc.

Defensively, several of your opponents have adopted upside down attitude signals, one or two are leading third and fifth best, but all of this will be noted. So what is the difference?

The difference is that there are 50 play problems and 50 defensive problems. Furthermore, these problems are matched. Let me explain.

The book is divided into four sections. Section I contains 25 play problems and Section II contains 25 defensive problems. Section III contains 25 defensive problems and Section IV 25 play problems.

Sections I and II have matched hands as do Sections III and IV. For example, play hand (1) finds you declaring 3NT. Defensive hand (1) in Section II finds you defending 3NT. Not only are the contracts the same, but the hands themselves are quite similar. You will be asked to defeat a 3NT contract in Section II that you have just made in Section I!

Of course, a card here or there has been changed to allow you to both make and defeat the contract if you play properly.

The same thinking applies when you come to Sections III and IV. For example, you must try to find a way to defeat 4 ♠ on hand (40) from Section III. Later you will be asked to play a very similar 4 ♠ in hand (40) from Section IV.

The trick is to remember how you either made or defeated these contracts so that you can either defeat or make them when they come up in different guises later. Furthermore, it is not going to be all that easy to recognize the hand. Some suits and some spot cards have been changed, but the basic idea remains the same—to show you how interrelated play and defense are; looking at the same hand from different points of view.

A special thanks to Ron Garber and Phil Isaacs for proofreading the book and along with everything else finding spot card errors—even after I told them not to bother checking for spot card errors. That was one area I *knew* was perfect!

And, oh yes, most important of all is to laugh at the jokes. Are you smiling? Good.

Edwin B. Kantar
Los Angeles

CONTENTS

SECTION I (PLAY HANDS)

SECTION II (DEFENSIVE HANDS)

SECTION III (DEFENSIVE HANDS)

SECTION IV (PLAY HANDS)

Section I
PLAY

(1) TRAP PASS

Both sides vulnerable
Dealer East

North
♠ K 10 2
♡ K J
♢ K Q 10 4 3 2
♣ J 4

South
♠ A Q J
♡ Q 9 8 7
♢ J 9
♣ K 5 3 2

East	South	West	North
1 ♣	Pass	Pass	1 ♢
Pass	2 NT	Pass	3 NT
Pass	Pass	Pass	

Opening lead: ♣ 10

You play the ♣ J from dummy and East plays the ♣ Q. Plan the play.

TRAP PASS (Solution)

North
♠ K 10 2
♡ K J
◊ K Q 10 4 3 2
♣ J 4

West	East
♠ 7 6 5	♠ 9 8 4 3
♡ 10 5 3 2	♡ A 6 4
◊ 8 6	◊ A 7 5
♣ 10 9 8 7	♣ A Q 6

South
♠ A Q J
♡ Q 9 8 7
◊ J 9
♣ K 5 3 2

Duck the ♣ Q. Your only chance to make this hand is if East, marked with every missing high card, has opened a three card suit.

Duck the first club and you limit East-West to two club tricks plus the two red aces.

Win the first club and you lose three clubs plus the two red aces.

KEY LESSON POINTERS

1. IF YOU MUST ASSUME THAT YOUR OPPONENT HAS OPENED A THREE CARD MINOR SUIT IN ORDER TO MAKE THE CONTRACT, DO SO.
2. A SHORT CLUB OPENING IS MORE LIKELY THAN A SHORT DIAMOND OPENING.
3. SHORT DIAMOND OPENINGS ARE USUALLY MADE WITH ONLY ONE DISTRIBUTION—4-4-3-2. (FOUR-FOUR IN THE MAJORS). SHORT CLUB OPENINGS ARE MADE WITH THREE DISTRIBUTIONS—4-4-2-3, 4-3-3-3, AND 3-4-3-3. WITH 3-3-4-3, THE PROPER OPENING BID IS ONE DIAMOND.
4. A HOLD UP PLAY WITH THE KING AFTER THE ACE HAS BEEN PLAYED IS A RELATIVELY COMMON PLAY. A HOLD UP PLAY WITH THE KING BEFORE THE ACE HAS BEEN PLAYED IS A RELATIVELY RARE PLAY. YOU MUST BE SURE THE KING LIES OVER THE ACE—IF YOU WISH TO KEEP YOUR PRESENT PARTNER.

(2) OUCH!

Both sides vulnerable
Dealer South

North
♠ 8 4 3
♡ J 7 6
♢ A Q 8 4
♣ Q 10 9

South
♠ A K J 7 5 2
♡ A K
♢ K 3
♣ A J 2

South	West	North	East
2 ♣	Pass	2 ♢	Pass
2 ♠	Pass	3 ♠	Pass
4 ♣	Pass	4 ♢	Pass
4 NT	Pass	5 ♢	Pass
5 NT	Pass	6 ♣	Pass
6 ♠	Pass	Pass	Pass

Opening lead: ♡ 10

You win the ♡ A and plunk down the ♠ K. East discards a lower heart. How do you continue?

OUCH! (Solution)

North
♠ 8 4 3
♡ J 7 6
◊ A Q 8 4
♣ Q 10 9

West
♠ Q 10 9 6
♡ 10 9 8
◊ J 9 7
♣ 8 6 4

East
♠ —
♡ Q 5 4 3 2
◊ 10 6 5 2
♣ K 7 5 3

South
♠ A K J 7 5 2
♡ A K
◊ K 3
♣ A J 2

You don't need much at this point to make this hand. All you need is to find East with the ♣ K and West with 4-3-3-3 distribution!

Even then you have to be careful. Very careful. Cash the ♡ K, enter dummy via a low diamond to the queen (or overtake the ◊ K), and try the ♣ Q.

If East covers, win the ♣ A (nice play), cash two more clubs ending in dummy and ruff a heart. Return to dummy with a diamond and ruff a diamond.

Assuming West has politely followed to all of these cards, you and West are each down to three trumps. Exit with a low trump and take the last two tricks with the ♠ K J.

Now back up to that play of the ♣ Q. If East does not cover, unblock the ♣ J so that you can remain in dummy to repeat the finesse. If East ducks the ♣ 10 as well, ruff a heart, cash the ♣ A and play as before. Unblocking the ♣ J is crucial. If you do not, you will be short an entry to dummy to shorten yourself to West's trump length.

KEY LESSON POINTERS

1. AN UGLY TRUMP DIVISION CAN SOMETIMES BE OVERCOME BY REDUCING ONESELF TO THE SAME TRUMP LENGTH AS THE OPPONENT. IF YOU CAN REMOVE ALL OF HIS OTHER CARDS YOU WILL BE ABLE TO THROW HIM IN WITH A TRUMP AND FORCE A TRUMP RETURN.
2. WITH Q 10 9 IN DUMMY FACING AJx IN YOUR HAND, LEAD THE QUEEN AND, IF NOT COVERED, UNDERPLAY THE JACK IF YOU WISH TO CREATE AN ADDITIONAL DUMMY ENTRY.

(3) ONE SHORT

East-West vulnerable
Dealer South

North
♠ J 10
♡ J 7 3
◇ K Q J 5
♣ K 7 6 2

South
♠ A Q 5
♡ 10 9 5
◇ A 10 9 3
♣ A J 4

South	West	North	East
1 NT	Pass	3 NT	Pass
Pass	Pass		

Opening lead: ♣ 3

You play low from dummy and capture East's nine with the jack.

1. What is your general plan?

ONE SHORT (Solution)

North
♠ J 10
♡ J 7 3
◇ K Q J 5
♣ K 7 6 2

West	East
♠ K 7 6	♠ 9 8 4 3 2
♡ K 8 6	♡ A Q 4 2
◇ 8 4 2	◇ 7 6
♣ Q 10 8 3	♣ 9 5

South
♠ A Q 5
♡ 10 9 5
◇ A 10 9 3
♣ A J 4

1. There are two ways to attack this contract: (1) cross to a diamond and run the
   ♠ J. If it wins, you have your contract, if it loses, you must sweat out the likely
   heart shift. (2) cross to a diamond and lead a heart to the ten!

   This is what is known as a "muddying the waters" play. You "attack" your
   weakest suit and see what happens. What usually happens is that the
   opponents switch to your strongest suit!

   Even if the opponents reel off four heart tricks you can still fall back on the
   spade finesse.

   On the actual lie of the cards there is a good chance that West will win the
   heart and continue a club. But he may switch to a spade! If West returns a club
   you can win in dummy and try the spade finesse. If West has the ♠ K, he will
   have to be a clever fellow to revert back to hearts. In any case, you've done
   your best to throw him off the scent.

KEY LESSON POINTERS

1. WHEN IT IS LIKELY THAT THE OPPONENTS WILL SWITCH TO YOUR
   WEAKEST SUIT, SURPRISING RESULTS CAN BE OBTAINED BY LEADING
   THE SUIT YOURSELF.
2. IF YOU TRY THIS TECHNIQUE AND IT WORKS, LET ME HEAR FROM YOU.
   IF IT DOESN'T, I DON'T KNOW YOU.

(4) DEFENSIVE HOLD-UP PLAY *(1)

East-West vulnerable
Dealer South

North
♠ 10 9 5 4
♡ J 7 3
◇ A Q J
♣ Q J 7

South
♠ A K 7
♡ Q 9
◇ K 10 5 2
♣ A 8 6 3

South	West	North	East
1 NT	Pass	3 NT	Pass
Pass	Pass		

Opening lead: ♡ 4

East wins the ♡ A and returns the ♡ 8 to your ♡ Q, West playing the ♡ 2. At trick three you lead the ♠ A and West plays the ♠ J.

1. What do you play at trick four?

You cash the ♠ K and West discards a low club.

2. Now what?

*Numbers in parenthesis *after* the title of the problem indicate that those numbered questions will be answered directly under the question. If you wish to work out the answer for yourself, do not read below the question prematurely.

DEFENSIVE HOLD-UP PLAY (Solution)

North

♠ 10 9 5 4
♡ J 7 3
◇ A Q J
♣ Q J 7

West	East
♠ J	♠ Q 8 6 3 2
♡ K 10 6 4 2	♡ A 8 5
◇ 9 7 6	◇ 8 4 3
♣ K 10 4 2	♣ 9 5

South

♠ A K 7
♡ Q 9
◇ K 10 5 2
♣ A 8 6 3

2. Play three rounds of diamonds ending in dummy. If West started with three diamonds or less, throw him in with a heart. After he cashes his three heart winners he will have to lead a club. You make the hand regardless of the location of the ♣ K.

   If West started with four or more diamonds, take the club finesse. This line of play assumes that West started with five hearts, based on the opening lead and the return.

KEY LESSON POINTERS

1. A PLAY THAT IS OFTEN OVERLOOKED BY YOUR PARTNERS (NOT YOU, OF COURSE), IS THE THROW-IN. AFTER STRIPPING A DANGEROUS OPPONENT (WEST) OF HIS SAFE EXIT CARDS—SPADES AND DIAMONDS—YOU CAN PUT HIM ON LEAD WITH HIS OWN SUIT AND PATIENTLY AWAIT THE FORCED RETURN IN THE FOURTH SUIT. PARTNER IS SURE TO BE IMPRESSED.

(5) QUICK ESTABLISHMENT

East-West vulnerable
Dealer South

North
♠ 9 8 7
♡ J 2
◇ K Q 3
♣ A J 6 5 4

South
♠ A 10
♡ A K 9 5
◇ J 10 8 7 6 5
♣ 3

South	West	North	East
1 ◇	Pass	2 ♣	Pass
2 ◇	Pass	3 ◇	Pass
3 ♡	Pass	4 ◇	Pass
5 ◇	Pass	Pass	Pass

Opening lead: ♠ 3

East plays the ♠ Q losing to your ace. You play the ♡ A K and ruff a heart low in dummy when West follows with the ♡ 6, ♡ 10 and ♡ Q.

Things are looking pretty good so you try a high diamond from dummy which holds, both following. Now what?

QUICK ESTABLISHMENT (Solution)

North
♠ 9 8 7
♡ J 2
♢ K Q 3
♣ A J 6 5 4

West
♠ J 5 4 3 2
♡ Q 10 6
♢ A 9 2
♣ 9 7

East
♠ K Q 6
♡ 8 7 4 3
♢ 4
♣ K Q 10 8 2

South
♠ A 10
♡ A K 9 5
♢ J 10 8 7 6 5
♣ 3

Lead a spade. The danger in leading dummy's remaining trump is that West, with both remaining trumps, will win the ace, lead a spade to his partner and ruff the heart return.

You can stop all this nonsense if you lead a spade—now! Once the communications between the defending hands have been snipped, there is no danger of losing your established heart winner.

KEY LESSON POINTERS

1. HAVING AN ESTABLISHED WINNER (♡ 9) IS NOT ENOUGH. YOU MUST KNOW HOW TO PROTECT IT WHEN THE TRUMP SUIT IS NOT SOLID.
2. THERE ARE THREE WAYS TO PROTECT AN ESTABLISHED WINNER THAT IS IN DANGER OF BEING RUFFED: (1) DISCARD IT ON ANOTHER ESTAB- LISHED WINNER; (2) RUFF IT—IF YOUR TRUMPS ARE STRONG ENOUGH; (3) CUT THE COMMUNICATIONS BETWEEN THE DEFENDERS' HANDS BY CONCEDING AN INEVITABLE LOSER WHILE YOU STILL HAVE TRUMP(S) IN DUMMY.

(6) MISSING KING

Neither side vulnerable
Dealer South

North
♠ Q 10 9 8 2
♡ K 6 3
◇ A 9 8
♣ 7 5

South
♠ A K 7 6 4 3
♡ A 4
◇ Q 7 6
♣ 10 4

South	West	North	East
1♠	2♣	3♠	4♣
4♠	Pass	Pass	Pass

Opening lead: ♣ K

East wins the second club with the ace and shifts to the ♡ Q. Trumps are 1-1. Plan the play. (If you play three rounds of hearts, both follow, East playing the ♡ J on the third round.)

MISSING KING (Solution)

North
♠ Q 10 9 8 2
♡ K 6 3
◇ A 9 8
♣ 7 5

West	East
♠ J	♠ 5
♡ 9 8 7	♡ Q J 10 5 2
◇ K J 5	◇ 10 4 3 2
♣ K Q J 9 8 2	♣ A 6 3

South
♠ A K 7 6 4 3
♡ A 4
◇ Q 7 6
♣ 10 4

This hand revolves around the location of the ◇ K. As always, whenever you have a touchy card combination to deal with, strip the hand before attacking the suit.

After the stripping process you must decide who is more likely to hold the relevant honor. In this case the clues point to West. If West had no honors outside of his main suit, clubs, he probably would have made a weak jump overcall.

Your plan should be to run the ◇ 8 into the West hand. After West wins the trick he will be endplayed.

You have a problem if East covers. If East has both the ◇ 10 and ◇ J, you must duck, endplaying East. However, if East has made a genius play of covering with 10xx(x) or Jxx(x) you must cover with the ◇ Q and later finesse the ◇ 9.

KEY LESSON POINTERS

1. IN ORDER TO LOCATE A KEY CARD GO BACK TO THE BIDDING.
2. A PLAYER WHO MAKES A SIMPLE OVERCALL MISSING THE ACE OR KING OF HIS PRESUMED SIX CARD SUIT, WILL GENERALLY HAVE AN OUTSIDE ACE OR KING. IF NOT, HE PROBABLY WOULD HAVE MADE A PREEMPTIVE JUMP OVERCALL.
3. IF POSSIBLE, STRIP THE HAND BEFORE ATTACKING THE CRITICAL SUIT.
4. NEVER ASSUME YOUR OPPONENTS ARE MAKING BRILLIANT PLAYS— BUT DON'T TELL THEM THAT.

(7) DOUBLE FIT

East-West vulnerable
Dealer West

North
♠ K J 9 5
♡ Q 2
◇ K Q 9 2
♣ 10 7 4

South
♠ 4 3
♡ A K J 10 9
◇ A J 10 3
♣ J 2

West	North	East	South
Pass	Pass	Pass	1 ♡
Pass	1 ♠	Pass	2 ◇
Pass	3 ◇	Pass	3 ♡
Pass	4 ♡	Pass	Pass
Pass			

Opening lead: ♣ K

East signals with the ♣ 9 and West continues with the ♣ A and a third club to East's ♣ Q which you ruff.
How do you continue?

DOUBLE FIT (Solution)

North
♠ K J 9 5
♡ Q 2
◊ K Q 9 2
♣ 10 7 4

West
♠ Q 7 6 2
♡ 8 3
◊ 6 5 4
♣ A K 5 3

East
♠ A 10 8
♡ 7 6 5 4
◊ 8 7
♣ Q 9 8 6

South
♠ 4 3
♡ A K J 10 9
◊ A J 10 3
♣ J 2

It is not enough to work out that East must have the ♠ A. (West, a passed hand, has already turned up with the ♣ A K.) You must develop your tenth trick in spades *before* drawing trumps.

If you draw trumps before you tackle spades, and you run into a normal 4-2 trump division, you will, in effect, be playing the hand in notrump. When you finally lead a spade to the jack and ace, East may produce a fourth club. Now wouldn't that be lovely when you have no more trumps?

No, the answer is to lead a spade to the jack at trick three. If it drives out the ace, as you suspect, East will be helpless. A club return can be ruffed in dummy, and no other return can prevent you from taking the balance.

KEY LESSON POINTERS

1. COUNT YOUR SURE TRICKS BEFORE EMBARKING ON THE PLAY.
2. IF YOU MUST DEVELOP AN EXTRA TRICK OR TWO, DECIDE WHETHER OR NOT YOU CAN AFFORD TO DRAW TRUMPS FIRST.
3. WHEN THERE IS A DANGER OF RUNNING OUT OF TRUMPS BY BEING FORCED IN A SUIT IN WHICH BOTH YOU AND DUMMY ARE VOID, IT USUALLY PAYS TO DEVELOP EXTRA TRICKS BEFORE DRAWING TRUMPS. USE THE DUMMY'S TRUMPS TO PROTECT YOU FROM RE-PEATED FORCES.

(8) WHAT ARE THEY TRYING TO DO TO YOU?

East-West vulnerable
Dealer South

North
♠ K 10
♡ A K 5 3
♢ Q 10 8 6
♣ 10 8 3

South
♠ Q J 9 8 4
♡ J 9
♢ K J 2
♣ 6 4 2

South	West	North	East
Pass	Pass	1 ♡	1 NT*
2 ♠	Pass	Pass	Pass

*16-18

Opening lead: ♣ K

East overtakes and shifts to ace and a diamond. Your move.

WHAT ARE THEY TRYING TO DO TO YOU?
(Solution)

North
♠ K 10
♡ A K 5 3
◇ Q 10 8 6
♣ 10 8 3

West
♠ 6 3 2
♡ 7 6 4 2
◇ 9 7 5 4
♣ K 5

East
♠ A 7 5
♡ Q 10 8
◇ A 3
♣ A Q J 9 7

South
♠ Q J 9 8 4
♡ J 9
◇ K J 2
♣ 6 4 2

It should be clear what East has in mind. East has the ♠ A and is planning to give West a third round club ruff in order to ruff a diamond.

To circumvent this diabolical plot, play the ace-king and a heart discarding a club. If East wins the trick (he may have to, or he may have forgotten to unblock) you are safe.

When East plays a third club, ruff high and play a trump to the king. If trumps are 3-3 you cannot be beaten. If trumps are 4-2 East can win the second spade and force you with a club to defeat you, but what other chance do you have?

KEY LESSON POINTERS

1. GIVE AN OPPONENT CREDIT FOR HAVING SOMETHING IN MIND WHEN HE MAKES AN UNUSUAL PLAY—UNLESS IT IS A FORMER PARTNER.
2. IN ORDER TO AVOID HAVING ONE OF YOUR WINNERS RUFFED AWAY, IT MAY BE NECESSARY TO SEVER COMMUNICATIONS BETWEEN THE OPPOSING HANDS.
3. ONE WAY OF CUTTING COMMUNICATIONS IS TO SUBSTITUTE ONE LOSER FOR ANOTHER WITH THE INTENTION OF KEEPING THE DANGER HAND (IN THIS INSTANCE, WEST) FROM GETTING THE LEAD. THE NAME OF THIS PLAY IS THE SCISSORS COUP.

(9) SIMPLICITY

Neither side vulnerable
Dealer North

North
♠ Q
♡ K Q 7 6
◇ A K J 7 3
♣ K 9 5

South
♠ A 10 9 8 7 6 5
♡ 3 2
◇ 4
♣ Q 10 2

North	East	South	West
1 ◇	Pass	1 ♠	Pass
2 ♡	Pass	2 ♠	Pass
2 NT	Pass	4 ♠	Pass
Pass	Pass		

Opening lead: ♡ J

You cover and East wins. East shifts to the ♣ 8, West wins the
♣ A and continues a club, East following. Plan the play from
here.

SIMPLICITY (Solution)

North
♠ Q
♡ K Q 7 6
◇ A K J 7 3
♣ K 9 5

West	East
♠ K 3 2	♠ J 4
♡ J 10 9	♡ A 8 5 4
◇ 10 6	◇ Q 9 8 5 2
♣ A J 6 4 3	♣ 8 7

South
♠ A 10 9 8 7 6 5
♡ 3 2
◇ 4
♣ Q 10 2

Play the ◇ A K and discard a club, then run the ♠ Q. You are being threatened with a club ruff. If West has the ♠ K and you do not get rid of your high club you may get it ruffed off. Lovely.

KEY LESSON POINTERS

1. DISCARDING A WINNER TO AVOID A RUFF IS A COMMON STRATEGY.
2. THE BEST PLAY FOR ONE LOSER WITH A SINGLETON QUEEN FACING A109xxxx IS TO RUN THE QUEEN.

(10) TELLING ALL (1)

Both sides vulnerable
Dealer South

North
♠ 9 7 6
♡ 10 7 6
♢ J 10 8
♣ A K 7 5

South
♠ A K Q 10
♡ A K 8 5 4
♢ 9 7
♣ Q 8

South	West	North	East
1 ♡	Pass	2 ♡	Pass
2 ♠	Pass	3 ♣	Pass
4 ♡	Pass	Pass	Pass

Opening lead: ♢ K

West continues with the ♢ 2 to East's ace and East plays a third diamond which you ruff low, West following with the ♢ Q.
At trick four you lead the ♡ A and East plays the ♡ Q.
1. What do you play at trick five?
    You lead a low heart. West wins the ♡ J, East discarding a diamond. West counters with a fourth diamond.
2. How do you handle this and what is your plan?

TELLING ALL (Solution)

North
♠ 9 7 6
♡ 10 7 6
♢ J 10 8
♣ A K 7 5

West
♠ 8 5 2
♡ J 9 3 2
♢ K Q 6 2
♣ 9 4

East
♠ J 4 3
♡ Q
♢ A 5 4 3
♣ J 10 6 3 2

South
♠ A K Q 10
♡ A K 8 5 4
♢ 9 7
♣ Q 8

2. Discard a spade from dummy and ruff in your hand. Obviously, you cannot afford to ruff in dummy. If you do, West will have a natural trump trick.

   At this point you remain with a high trump in each hand while West has two trumps. Not a very healthy situation.

   West is known to have started with four hearts and four diamonds. As the hand cannot be made if West has a black singleton, assume he is 3-2 in the black suits.

   Begin by playing the ♠ A K Q. If West follows, cash two clubs and crossruff the last two tricks with high trumps. West will have to underruff.

   If West ruffs the third spade, overtrump, cross to the ♣ Q, draw West's last trump and take the balance.

   Finally, if West discards a club on the third spade, cash two clubs and crossruff. The key is to play spades before clubs. If you begin with three clubs West may ruff.

KEY LESSON POINTERS

1. HOLDING A K 8xx FACING 10xx, THE SAFETY PLAY FOR FOUR TRICKS IS TO PLAY THE ACE AND, IF AN HONOR DROPS FROM EITHER HAND OR THE NINE DROPS FROM LHO, LEAD LOW TOWARDS THE 10.
2. WHEN DECLARER AND DUMMY REMAIN WITH ONE HIGH TRUMP EACH AND ONE DEFENDER HAS TWO SMALLER TRUMPS, DECLARER MUST MAKE HIS TWO TRUMPS SEPARATELY—IF HE CANNOT AFFORD TO LOSE ANOTHER TRICK.

(11) SLAM TRY REFUSED (1)

Neither side vulnerable
Dealer East

North
♠ J 4 3 2
♡ A Q 8
◇ K J 6 5
♣ A 3

South
♠ K 6 5
♡ K J 4
◇ A Q 10 9 8 7
♣ 2

East	South	West	North
3 ♣	3 ◇	Pass	4 ♣
Pass	4 ◇	Pass	5 ◇
Pass	Pass	Pass	

Opening lead: ♣ 6

1. No, you can't get back to 3 NT. How do you plan to avoid the loss of three spade tricks?

   Strip the hand (both follow to three hearts, and East discards three clubs on three trump plays) and lead a low spade from dummy.

2. When you lead a low spade from dummy, East plays the ♠ 7. Which spade do you play? Why?

SLAM TRY REFUSED (Solution)

North
♠ J 4 3 2
♡ A Q 8
◇ K J 6 5
♣ A 3

West
♠ A 10 9
♡ 10 9 7 5
◇ 4 3 2
♣ 10 8 6

East
♠ Q 8 7
♡ 6 3 2
◇ —
♣ K Q J 9 7 5 4

South
♠ K 6 5
♡ K J 4
◇ A Q 10 9 8 7
♣ 2

2. Duck the ♠ 7. As the ♠ 7 is the lowest outstanding spade, West will have to win the trick and will be endplayed.

   If East had played the ♠ 8 you would have had a problem. It would be right to cover if West started with the A Q, but wrong to cover when East started with the queen and West the ace.

KEY LESSON POINTERS

1. WHEN YOU HAVE LOSERS IN ONLY ONE SUIT STRIP THE HAND, IF POSSIBLE, BEFORE ATTACKING THE SUIT.
2. WHEN YOU FINALLY ATTACK THE CRITICAL SUIT, TRY TO DUCK THE LEAD INTO THE NON-DANGER HAND. IN THIS CASE, WEST IS THE NON-DANGER HAND AS LONG AS YOU RETAIN THE ♠ K.

(12) ORDERLY

Both sides vulnerable
Dealer South

North
♠ A Q 6 4
♡ A Q 3
◇ A 5 4 3 2
♣ K

South
♠ K 8 7
♡ K 9 4 2
◇ K Q
♣ Q 8 3 2

South	West	North	East
1 ♣	Pass	1 ◇	Pass
1 ♡	Pass	1 ♠	Pass
1 NT	Pass	6 NT	Pass
Pass	Pass		

Opening lead: ♣ J

East wins the ♣ A and returns the ♣ 4 to your queen. What do you discard from dummy and in what order do you cash your winners?

ORDERLY (Solution)

North
♠ A Q 6 4
♡ A Q 3
◇ A 5 4 3 2
♣ K

West	East
♠ J 9 5 2	♠ 10 3
♡ 8 7 5	♡ J 10 6
◇ 7 6	◇ J 10 9 8
♣ J 10 9 7	♣ A 6 5 4

South
♠ K 8 7
♡ K 9 4 2
◇ K Q
♣ Q 8 3 2

Discard a heart from dummy. You cannot afford to discard a diamond. If diamonds break 3-3 you have twelve tricks. Similarly, a spade discard can cost the contract if that suit breaks 3-3.

Cash the ◇ K Q, cross to dummy with the ♡ A and cash the ◇ A discarding a spade or a club. If that suit does not break, cash the ♡ Q, reenter your hand with the ♠ K and cash the ♡ K. If hearts don't break you are not going to make your contract.

Assuming hearts break 3-3 (or the ♡ J 10 falls), cash the last heart and hope you are squeezing somebody. In this case you will be squeezing West who is holding both the spade and club guards.

KEY LESSON POINTERS

1. TRY TO LEAVE YOURSELF AS MANY OPTIONS AS POSSIBLE WHEN FORCED TO MAKE AN EARLY DISCARD.
2. WITH A LIKELY 11 TRICKS AND A POSSIBILITY OF A TWELFTH FROM ANY OF FOUR SUITS, A SQUEEZE IS QUITE LIKELY.
3. IN GENERAL, CASH TRICKS IN BLOCKED SUITS (DIAMONDS AND HEARTS) BEFORE CASHING WINNERS IN A SUIT THAT IS NOT BLOCKED (SPADES).

(13) HOPE

Both sides vulnerable
Dealer North

North
♠ 2
♡ A K 8 7
♢ 6 5
♣ K Q 10 6 4 3

South
♠ K Q J 10 9 8 7
♡ 5
♢ Q 10 9 8
♣ A

North	East	South	West
1 ♣	1 ♡	1 ♠	Pass
2 ♣	Pass	4 ♠	Pass
Pass	Pass		

Opening lead: ♡ 3

Plan the play.

HOPE (Solution)

North
♠ 2
♡ A K 8 7
◇ 6 5
♣ K Q 10 6 4 3

<table>
<tr><td>West</td><td>East</td></tr>
<tr><td>♠ 4 3</td><td>♠ A 6 5</td></tr>
<tr><td>♡ 6 4 3</td><td>♡ Q J 10 9 2</td></tr>
<tr><td>◇ K J 7 4</td><td>◇ A 3 2</td></tr>
<tr><td>♣ 8 7 5 2</td><td>♣ J 9</td></tr>
</table>

South
♠ K Q J 10 9 8 7
♡ 5
◇ Q 10 9 8
♣ A

Simple enough. Play the ♡ A K and then discard the ♣ A. That should raise some eyebrows. Next, cash the ♣ K Q and discard two diamonds. If all of this lives, you have ten tricks, six spades, two hearts and two clubs.

KEY LESSON POINTERS

1. UNBLOCKING ACES IS ALWAYS IMPRESSIVE. IN THIS CASE IT WAS THE ONLY WAY TO LIBERATE THE ♣ K Q.
2. IF YOU BLEW THIS ONE, READ THROUGH THIS BOOK SLOWLY—VERY SLOWLY.

(14) ENTRYLESS DUMMY?

North-South vulnerable
Dealer North

North
♠ A K 8
♡ 6 4 3
◇ Q 5 4
♣ 6 5 4 3

South
♠ —
♡ A K Q J 10 8 2
◇ A 9 2
♣ Q J 10

North	East	South	West
Pass	1 ♣	4 ♡	Pass
Pass	Pass		

Opening lead: ♣ 2

East wins the ♣ A K and returns a third club, West following. At trick four you cash the ♡ A and West discards the ♠ 7.
1. What is East's distribution?
2. How do you continue?

ENTRYLESS DUMMY? (Solution)

North
♠ A K 8
♡ 6 4 3
◇ Q 5 4
♣ 6 5 4 3

<table>
<tr><td>

West
♠ 10 7 6 5 4 2
♡ —
◇ 10 8 7 6
♣ 8 7 2
</td><td>

East
♠ Q J 9 3
♡ 9 7 5
◇ K J 3
♣ A K 9
</td></tr>
</table>

South
♠ —
♡ A K Q J 10 8 2
◇ A 9 2
♣ Q J 10

1. 4-3-3-3. With 3-3-4-3, he would open 1 ◇.
2. Cash a second heart and exit with the ♡ 2! East will be forced to win the trick and the ball game is over. If East returns a spade you discard both diamonds on the top spades and, if East leads a diamond, run it to your queen.

   By giving East a trump trick you get two tricks in return. Not a bad deal.

KEY LESSON POINTERS

1. WHEN THE DUMMY HAS WINNERS WITH NO APPARENT ENTRY, PERHAPS YOU CAN FORCE THE OPPONENTS TO PUT YOU IN THE DUMMY. ONE WAY IS TO THROW THEM IN WITH A TRUMP—EVEN IF IT MEANS CREATING A TRUMP LOSER!
2. IF YOUR PARTNER DOESN'T SAY "NICE PLAY" AFTER THIS ONE, CHANGE PARTNERS.

(15) BLACK TWO-SUITER

Neither side vulnerable
Dealer South

North
♠ J 10 3
♡ K Q
♢ K Q 9 4
♣ J 6 5 4

South
♠ A K 9 8 7
♡ 10 2
♢ 3
♣ A Q 7 3 2

South	West	North	East
1 ♣	Pass	1 ♢	Pass
1 ♠	Pass	2 NT	Pass
3 ♠	Pass	4 ♠	Pass
Pass	Pass		

Opening lead: ♢ J

You cover and East wins the ♢ A and shifts to the ♣ 8. Fearing a singleton, you rise with the ♣ A, cash the ♠ A and lead a heart to dummy with the intention of finessing the spade.
1. Do you think you have played the hand properly so far?
2. If not, what would you have done differently?

BLACK TWO-SUITER (Solution)

North
♠ J 10 3
♡ K Q
♢ K Q 9 4
♣ J 6 5 4

<table>
<tr><td>

West
♠ 4 2
♡ A 8 7 6
♢ J 10 8 7
♣ K 10 9

</td><td>

East
♠ Q 6 5
♡ J 9 5 4 3
♢ A 6 5 2
♣ 8

</td></tr>
</table>

South
♠ A K 9 8 7
♡ 10 2
♢ 3
♣ A Q 7 3 2

1. No.
2. You should duck the opening lead to make it harder for East to make a potentially damaging club shift. If the ♢ J holds, the best the defenders can do is play ace and a heart. You win and run the ♠ J. If it wins, continue spades, eventually conceding a club. If the ♠ J loses, you can use the ♠ 10 as entry to finesse the club.

   True, East can overtake partner's ♢ J and shift to a club at trick two, but ducking the opening lead makes that play a bit harder, to say the least.

KEY LESSON POINTERS

1. WHEN APPREHENSIVE OF A SHIFT FROM A PARTICULAR PLAYER, MAKE IT DIFFICULT FOR THAT PLAYER TO GET THE LEAD.
2. SOME PLAYERS OPEN 5-5 BLACK TWO-SUITERS WITH ONE CLUB, OTHERS, ONE SPADE, AND YET ANOTHER GROUP VARIES THE OPENING BID DEPENDING UPON HONOR STRENGTH AND SUIT TEXTURE. DISCUSS THIS WITH YOUR PARTNER.

(16) HUGE LEAP

North-South vulnerable
Dealer West

North
♠ 6
♡ 8 4 3
◇ K 7 6 4 2
♣ K Q 6 5

South
♠ A K Q J 8 7 5
♡ A Q 9
◇ A 9
♣ 8

West	North	East	South
3♣	Pass	Pass	6♠
Pass	Pass	Pass	

Opening lead: ◇ 3

You play low from dummy and capture East's ten. East has three trumps, West two. Plan the play.

HUGE LEAP (Solution)

North
♠ 6
♡ 8 4 3
◇ K 7 6 4 2
♣ K Q 6 5

West
♠ 9 3
♡ K 10 2
◇ 3
♣ A J 10 9 4 3 2

East
♠ 10 4 2
♡ J 7 6 5
◇ Q J 10 8 5
♣ 7

South
♠ A K Q J 8 7 5
♡ A Q 9
◇ A 9
♣ 8

Draw trumps, retaining at least two hearts and three clubs on the table and lead your club.

If West wins, you have the rest, no problem. However, if West makes the stronger play of ducking, win in dummy and lead a heart to the *nine*.

Assuming this loses to the ten or jack, West will be endplayed if he has no more diamonds. A heart return goes into your A Q and plunking down the ♣ A won't help. You can ruff, enter dummy with a diamond and discard the ♡ Q on a winning club.

If West produces a diamond upon winning the heart, you are reduced to the heart finesse. Cheer up. If West has a second diamond, his original distribution is likely to be 2-1-3-7, which means the heart finesse will work.

KEY LESSON POINTERS

1. WITH A Q 9 OPPOSITE TWO OR THREE SMALL CARDS, THE BEST PLAY FOR TWO TRICKS IS TO LEAD LOW TO THE NINE AND THEN LOW TO THE QUEEN.
2. TRY TO WORK OUT THE LIKELY DISTRIBUTION OF YOUR OPPONENTS' HANDS, NOT ONLY FROM THE BIDDING AND THE LEAD, BUT FROM THE WAY THE PLAY DEVELOPS AS WELL.

(17) ACHILLES HEEL DISCOVERED

North-South vulnerable
Dealer West

North
♠ K 9 8 7 6
♡ Q 4
◇ K 10 5
♣ K 10 5

South
♠ 2
♡ A K J 10 5 3 2
◇ A 8
♣ 6 4 2

West	North	East	South
1 ♣	1 ♠	Pass	4 ♡
Pass	Pass	Pass	

Opening lead: ♣ Q

Which club do you play from dummy? Why?

ACHILLES HEEL DISCOVERED (Solution)

North
♠ K 9 8 7 6
♡ Q 4
♢ K 10 5
♣ K 10 5

West	East
♠ A Q J	♠ 10 5 4 3
♡ 9 8	♡ 7 6
♢ Q 9 3	♢ J 7 6 4 2
♣ Q J 9 7 3	♣ A 8

South
♠ 2
♡ A K J 10 5 3 2
♢ A 8
♣ 6 4 2

Low. West is unlikely to be underleading the ♣ A. The greater danger is that East is short in clubs and the opponents will realize a club ruff.

If East has a doubleton ♣ A, and you cover the opening lead, East will win and may return his remaining club with the speed of summer lightning. Most West players will now find a third club play. Down one.

If you duck the opening lead and the cards are distributed as you see, West does best to play a second club to East's now blank ♣ A. East must return a spade, not a diamond, to realize a club ruff. Will East know to do this?

Of course, an expert West will tell East which suit to return by the size of the club he leads at trick two—but you may not be playing against experts. After all, not everyone defends as well as you.

KEY LESSON POINTERS

1. DO NOT ASSUME THE LEAD OF THE QUEEN VS. A SUIT CONTRACT IS FROM AN AQJ COMBINATION.
2. WHEN THE QUEEN IS LED VS. A SUIT CONTRACT AND THE KING IS IN DUMMY, IT IS USUALLY RIGHT TO PLAY LOW FROM DUMMY. IF THIRD HAND HAS Ax OR Axx YOU MAY BE ABLE TO FLUSH OUT THE ACE WITHOUT PLAYING THE KING.

DUMMY

♣ K 7 6 5

West	East
♣ Q J 10 9 3	♣ A 8 2

South

♣ 4

WEST LEADS THE ♣ Q. PLAY LOW FROM DUMMY. IF WEST CONTINUES THE SUIT, PLAY LOW AGAIN. LATER YOU CAN RUFF A CLUB, ESTABLISHING THE KING.

(18) WHICH FINESSE?

North-South vulnerable
Dealer West

North

♠ A Q 4 3
♡ A Q 7
♢ A Q J 10 2
♣ 8

South

♠ J 5 2
♡ 10 9 5
♢ K 8 7 5
♣ K J 9

West	North	East	South
Pass	1 ♢	Pass	1 NT
2 ♣	2 ♠	Pass	3 ♢
Pass	3 ♡	Pass	3 NT
Pass	Pass	Pass	

Opening lead: ♣ 6

East plays the ♣ 2 and you win the ♣ 9. What is your plan and what do you play to trick two?

WHICH FINESSE? (Solution)

North
♠ A Q 4 3
♡ A Q 7
♢ A Q J 10 2
♣ 8

West	East
♠ K 10 8	♠ 9 7 6
♡ J 4 2	♡ K 8 6 3
♢ 9	♢ 6 4 3
♣ A Q 10 6 5 3	♣ 7 4 2

South
♠ J 5 2
♡ 10 9 5
♢ K 8 7 5
♣ K J 9

You must decide which major suit finesse to take. Furthermore, you have to make up your mind before you cash your diamonds because you cannot return to your hand if you cash all five diamonds.

Psychologically, your best bet is to lead the ♠ J at once and watch West's reaction. Many players cover an honor with an honor as if it were a religious obligation. If West is one of these players, you are in great shape.

If West covers the ♠ J you have nine tricks. If West plays low without a care in the world, you can rise with the ♠ A and take the heart finesse instead.

KEY LESSON POINTERS

1. WHEN YOU MUST DECIDE BETWEEN ONE OF TWO FINESSES AND YOU CAN LEAD A TEMPTING HONOR IN ONE OF THE TWO SUITS, DO IT. IT MAY BE COVERED. IF IT ISN'T, YOU CAN ALWAYS REFUSE THAT FINESSE AND TAKE THE OTHER.
2. MAKE YOUR "BIG" PLAYS EARLY BEFORE THE DEFENDERS CAN COUNT YOUR TRICKS AND/OR GET EMOTIONALLY SETTLED.

(19) JACK DENIES (1)

East-West vulnerable
Dealer North

North
♠ A 10 4
♡ Q J 9 7 6
◇ K Q
♣ A Q 2

South
♠ Q 6 5
♡ 5 4
◇ A J 10 4 3 2
♣ 7 4

North	East	South	West
1 ♡	Pass	1 NT	Pass
3 NT	Pass	Pass	Pass

Opening lead: ♣ J (Denies a higher honor)

1. Which club do you play from dummy?
   You play the ♣ A and East plays the ♣ 8.
2. What do you play now?

JACK DENIES (Solution)

North
♠ A 10 4
♡ Q J 9 7 6
◇ K Q
♣ A Q 2

West	East
♠ J 9 7	♠ K 8 3 2
♡ A 10	♡ K 8 3 2
◇ 8 7 5	◇ 9 6
♣ J 10 9 5 3	♣ K 8 6

South
♠ Q 6 5
♡ 5 4
◇ A J 10 4 3 2
♣ 7 4

2. A low spade. If East has the ♠ K, he may play low in which case you have stolen your ninth trick. If East wins the ♠ K and mistakenly shifts to a diamond, you also have nine tricks.

Finally, East may have ♣ Kx in which case you still have good chances even if the ♠ Q loses to West.

KEY LESSON POINTERS

1. KNOW YOUR OPPONENTS' LEAD CONVENTIONS. WHEN THEY PLAY "JACK DENIES" AND YOU HAVE THE ACE AND QUEEN BETWEEN YOUR HAND AND DUMMY, IT DOESN'T TAKE A GENIUS TO FIGURE OUT WHO HAS THE KING.
2. WHEN YOU HOLD A CONCEALED SOLID SUIT, MAKE YOUR DARING PLAYS EARLY BEFORE EITHER OPPONENT CAN COUNT YOUR LONG SUIT TRICKS.
3. THE PROPER PLAY FOR TWO TRICKS WITH A 10x FACING Qxx, IS LOW TO THE QUEEN. IF THE QUEEN LOSES TO THE KING, LEAD LOW TO THE TEN.

(20) COMPETITIVE BIDDING

Neither side vulnerable
Dealer East

North
♠ Q 5 3
♡ K
◊ A K Q J 8 3
♣ J 9 5

South
♠ K J 9 8 4
♡ Q 10 6
◊ 10 5 4
♣ Q 3

East	South	West	North
1 ♣	Pass	1 ♡	2 ◊
2 ♡	2 ♠	Pass	Pass
3 ♡	Pass	Pass	3 ♠
Pass	Pass	Pass	

Opening lead: ♣ 2

East wins the two top clubs, West playing the ♣ 7 and shifts to the ♡ 7. West wins the ♡ A and returns the ♣ 6 to dummy's jack as you discard the ♡ 10.

At trick five you lead a low spade to the jack which holds. Now what?

COMPETITIVE BIDDING (Solution)

North
♠ Q 5 3
♡ K
◇ A K Q J 8 3
♣ J 9 5

West	East
♠ 10 7 6	♠ A 2
♡ A 9 8 3 2	♡ J 7 5 4
◇ 7 6	◇ 9 2
♣ 7 6 2	♣ A K 10 8 4

South
♠ K J 9 8 4
♡ Q 10 6
◇ 10 5 4
♣ Q 3

Cross to dummy with a diamond and lead another low spade. You are faced with three possible dangers: (1) East holding ♠ A10xx; (2) a diamond ruff; (3) East holding ♠ Ax and promoting West's ♠ 10 by leading a fourth club if you lead a spade to the queen.

Of these three dangers, the third is the most likely. If there was a diamond ruff available, East or West would have shifted to the suit eons ago.

If East has ♠ A10xx, the bidding and the lead would have been different. For example, if East started with 4-4-2-3 distribution, West would have started with five clubs and would not have led the ♣ 2. Nor is it likely that East would have raised hearts twice with 4-3-2-4 distribution.

No, the real danger is an enemy trump promotion. You can avoid this by leading a second *low* spade from dummy.

KEY LESSON POINTERS

1. DO NOT GUARD AGAINST NON-EXISTENT DANGERS. GUARD ONLY AGAINST THOSE THAT ARE CONSISTENT WITH THE BIDDING AND DEFENSE.
2. TO AVOID A TRUMP PROMOTION PLAY WHEN MISSING THE HIGH TRUMP, IT MAY BE NECESSARY TO LEAD LOW TWICE TOWARDS YOUR OWN TRUMP HOLDING WITHOUT SQUANDERING AN HONOR FROM DUMMY.

(21) COMING THRU (1)

North-South vulnerable
Dealer West

North
♠ K 4 2
♡ 8 7 4
◇ A Q J 10 4
♣ K Q

South
♠ J 3
♡ A K Q 9 3 2
◇ K 3 2
♣ J 5

West	North	East	South
Pass	1 NT	3 ♠	4 ♡
Pass	Pass	Pass	

Opening lead: ♠ 10

You play low from dummy and East plays the ♠ Q.
1. Which spade do you play?
    You try the ♠ J, but East is not fooled (maybe you took too long to play it!) and continues with the ♠ A, West discarding a low diamond.
    When East continues with a third spade, you ruff with the ♡ A, West discarding the ♣ 8. When you cash the ♡ K, West plays the ♡ J.
2. How do you continue?

COMING THRU (Solution)

North
♠ K 4 2
♡ 8 7 4
♢ A Q J 10 4
♣ K Q

West
♠ 10
♡ J 10
♢ 9 8 6 5
♣ A 8 7 6 4 3

East
♠ A Q 9 8 7 6 5
♡ 6 5
♢ 7
♣ 10 9 2

South
♠ J 3
♡ A K Q 9 3 2
♢ K 3 2
♣ J 5

2. Play the ♡ Q. It is more likely that hearts will divide 2-2 than it is that a silent West has two singletons.

KEY LESSON POINTERS

1. WHEN DECLARING, PLAY THE CARDS YOU ARE KNOWN TO HOLD AS SOON AS POSSIBLE. FOR EXAMPLE, YOU ARE MARKED WITH THE ♠ J FROM WEST'S LEAD OF THE ♠ 10. IF YOU PLAY THE ♠ 3 AT TRICK ONE, EAST WILL KNOW THAT YOU ARE THE ONE WITH THE REMAINING SPADE. IF YOU PLAY THE ♠ J, EAST MUST GUESS WHO HAS THE ♠ 3. YOU'RE SO TRICKY.

2. DO NOT PLAY A NON-VULNERABLE VS. VULNERABLE OPPONENT FOR TWO SINGLETONS IF HE HAS NOT MADE A PEEP DURING THE BIDDING.

(22) COPING

Neither side vulnerable
Dealer East

North
♠ A 4 3
♡ K Q 10
♢ J 9
♣ Q J 10 8 4

South
♠ K 10 6
♡ A J 4 2
♢ K Q 10
♣ 9 6 5

East	South	West	North
1 ♢	Pass	Pass	2 ♣
Pass	2 NT	Pass	3 NT
Pass	Pass	Pass	

Opening lead: ♢ 8

You play the ♢ J from dummy, East plays the ♢ 7 and you overtake in order to lead a low club at trick two. West wins the ♣ K and returns the ♢ 3. East wins and exits a diamond, West discarding a heart.
    Plan the play.

COPING (Solution)

North
♠ A 4 3
♡ K Q 10
◇ J 9
♣ Q J 10 8 4

West	East
♠ 9 8 7 2	♠ Q J 5
♡ 9 8 7 3	♡ 6 5
◇ 8 3	◇ A 7 6 5 4 2
♣ K 7 2	♣ A 3

South
♠ K 10 6
♡ A J 4 2
◇ K Q 10
♣ 9 6 5

East must have the ♣ A, so there is no point in playing a club in order to watch East reel off his diamond winners.

The better chance is to play East for both missing spade honors. Play four rounds of hearts, reducing all hands to five cards.

East will be forced to hold three spades, the ♣ A and, therefore, only *one* winning diamond. Now you can knock out the ♣ A for your ninth trick.

If, on the run of the hearts, East discards a spade and keeps two winning diamonds, play the ♠ A K and hope the Q J drops.

KEY LESSON POINTERS

1. WHEN ONE DEFENDER HAS ESTABLISHED WINNERS (DIAMONDS) PLUS TWO SIDE SUITS TO PROTECT (CLUBS AND SPADES), THE RUN OF A LONG SUIT MIGHT WELL DESTROY HIS HAND. HE IS USUALLY REDUCED TO A HOBSON'S CHOICE—EITHER DISCARD AN ESTAB-LISHED WINNER (OR TWO) OR LEAVE A SIDE SUIT UNPROTECTED.
2. MOST OPENING ONE BIDS SHOW AT LEAST 11 HIGH CARD POINTS. ONCE WEST PRODUCES THE ♣ K, DECLARER KNOWS THAT EAST HAS EVERY OTHER MISSING POINT.

(23) HEART BYPASS (1) (2)

East-West vulnerable
Dealer North

North
♠ A 7 4 2
♡ A J
◇ A 8 6 4 2
♣ 7 6

South
♠ K 8 3
♡ 9 7 4 2
◇ J 9 7
♣ A K Q

North	East	South	West
1 ◇	Pass	2 NT	Pass
3 NT	Pass	Pass	Pass

Opening lead: ♣ J (Denies a higher honor)

1. East plays the ♣ 2 at trick one. What card do you lead at trick two?

   You lead the ◇ 9 as a preliminary unblock. West plays the ◇ Q.
2. Which diamond to you play from dummy? Why?

   You win the ◇ A in case the ◇ Q is a singleton. If it is, you lose two diamond tricks if you win the ◇ A, three if you do not.

   After winning the ◇ A you play a diamond from dummy. East plays the ◇ K.
3. Which diamond do you play from your hand?

HEART BYPASS (Solution)

North
♠ A 7 4 2
♡ A J
◇ A 8 6 4 2
♣ 7 6

West	East
♠ J 9 6 5	♠ Q 10
♡ 6 5 3	♡ K Q 10 8
◇ Q	◇ K 10 5 3
♣ J 10 9 8 3	♣ 5 4 2

South
♠ K 8 3
♡ 9 7 4 2
◇ J 9 7
♣ A K Q

3. The ◇ J. As it is apparent that West has a singleton diamond, you are doomed to lose two diamond tricks in any event. If you play low, and East shifts to a heart, you lack the dummy entries to set up the diamonds for the three tricks you need in the suit.

   However, if you unblock the ◇ J, even a heart shift won't kill you if your ♡ 9 stands up as a fourth round stopper.

   Assume East shifts to a heart. You win in dummy and play the ◇ 8, underplaying the ◇ 7. East wins and is helpless. In fact, anytime East has four or more hearts, your ♡ 9 will stand up as a stopper.

KEY LESSON POINTERS

1. BE ON THE LOOKOUT FOR SUIT BLOCKS WHEN YOU ARE ESTABLISH-ING UNEVENLY DIVIDED SUITS (4-3, 5-3, 6-3) AND THE THREE CARD SUIT HAS HIGH INTERMEDIATE CARDS. IF THERE ARE ENTRY PROB-LEMS, UNBLOCK THE HIGH INTERMEDIATES FROM THE THREE CARD HOLDING AS SOON AS POSSIBLE.
2. HOLDING A J DOUBLETON IN DUMMY OPPOSITE 9xxx IN YOUR HAND, YOU HAVE A SECOND STOPPER IN THE SUIT WHENEVER YOUR RIGHT HAND OPPONENT ATTACKS THE SUIT AND HOLDS FOUR OR MORE CARDS IN THE SUIT.

(24) TEST THEM (1)

Neither side vulnerable
Dealer South

North
♠ K Q J 7
♡ 10 2
◇ K 10 9 8 2
♣ 6 5

South
♠ A 2
♡ K 7 6 5
◇ A J 7 5
♣ A J 9

South	West	North	East
1 NT	Pass	2 ♣	Pass
2 ♡	Pass	3 NT	Pass
Pass	Pass		

Opening lead: ♣ 2 (Third or fifth best)

1. East plays the ♣ K. Which club do you play, why?
      You win the ♣ A. You may have another stopper if East
   has the ♣ 10—or if you can keep East off lead.
2. How do you continue?

TEST THEM (Solution)

North
♠ K Q J 7
♡ 10 2
◇ K 10 9 8 2
♣ 6 5

West
♠ 9 6
♡ Q 9 4 3
◇ Q 3
♣ Q10 8 3 2

East
♠ 10 8 5 4 3
♡ A J 8
◇ 6 4
♣ K 7 4

South
♠ A 2
♡ A J 7 5
◇ K 7 6 5
♣ A J 9

1. Lead the ◇ J to the ◇ A and run the ◇ 10 into the non-danger hand, West. Obviously, you cannot afford to lose a diamond to East for fear of a club play.

    Even if the diamond finesse loses, you are still alive. If West has the ♡ A you are completely safe. Even if East has the ♡ A, West must find the heart shift. Furthermore, even if West finds the heart shift, East may win and return a heart rather than a club. So many chances to err.

KEY LESSON POINTERS

1. WHEN ONE DEFENDER IS KNOWN TO HOLD A LONG SUIT (WEST FIGURES TO HAVE FIVE CLUBS), THE OTHER DEFENDER IS MORE LIKELY TO HOLD LENGTH IN ANY OTHER SUIT—ANOTHER REASON TO PLAY EAST FOR THE ◇ Q.
2. EVEN THOUGH YOU MAY HAVE NO INTENTION OF FINESSING, LEAD THE HIGHEST HONOR CARD YOU CAN AFFORD TOWARDS A HIGHER HONOR. AN EXAMPLE IS LEADING THE ◇ J AT TRICK TWO. REMEMBER, SOME PLAYERS CONSIDER IT A MORAL OBLIGATION TO COVER AN HONOR WITH AN HONOR.
3. A J 9 FACING xx OR xxx IN THE DUMMY FREQUENTLY TRANSLATES INTO TWO WINNERS WHEN RIGHT HAND OPPONENT HAS BOTH HIGH HONORS OR ONE HIGH HONOR ALONG WITH THE TEN.

(25) NONFORCING JUMP REBID (1)

North-South vulnerable
Dealer South

North
♠ A 3
♡ J 4
♢ K Q 5 4 3 2
♣ 5 4 3

South
♠ K 2
♡ K 10 9
♢ A J 7
♣ Q J 10 7 6

South	West	North	East
1 ♣	Pass	1 ♢	Pass
1 NT	Pass	3 ♢	Pass
3 NT	Pass	Pass	Pass

Opening lead: ♠ Q

1. Where do you win this trick, and what is your plan?
   You win in dummy and lead the ♡ J.
2. When you lead the ♡ J, East plays low. Which heart do you play and why?

NONFORCING JUMP REBID (Solution)

North

♠ A 3
♡ J 4
♢ K Q 5 4 3 2
♣ 5 4 3

West	East
♠ Q J 9 8	♠ 10 7 6 5 4
♡ Q 8 7 6	♡ A 5 3 2
♢ 10 6	♢ 9 8
♣ A 9 2	♣ K 8

South

♠ K 2
♡ K 10 9
♢ A J 7
♣ Q J 10 7 6

2.   It's little more than a guess, however, the odds favor playing the king for two reasons:

   1.   Inexperienced players tend to cover honors with honors. If East is inexperienced, chances are you would be seeing the ♡ Q on the table.

   2.   If West has led from a five card suit (not clear), chances are he does not hold the ♡ A because he failed to overcall your 1 ♣ opening, not vulnerable vs. vulnerable,

   None of this is conclusive, of course, but when you are grasping at straws....

KEY LESSON POINTERS

1.   THERE ARE TWO WAYS TO ATTACK HANDS OF THIS TYPE: RUN THE LONG SUIT AND WATCH THE DISCARDS; LEAD A CRITICAL HONOR AT ONCE BEFORE THE OPPONENTS HAVE HAD A CHANCE TO COMPOSE THEMSELVES.

2.   IF YOU RUN THE LONG SUIT FIRST, MAKE SURE YOU HAVE ENOUGH CONVENIENT DISCARDS. HERE YOU ARE NOT TOO COMFORTABLE DISCARDING ON THE LAST DIAMOND.

3.   INEXPERIENCED PLAYERS TEND TO COVER AN HONOR WITH AN HONOR FAR MORE OFTEN THAN PLAYERS WHO COUNT TRICKS.

4.   WHEN VULNERABLE AGAINST NONVULNERABLE, ASSUME THE POSSI-BILITY OF RELATIVELY LIGHT ONE LEVEL MAJOR SUIT OVERCALLS. THE ABSENCE OF AN OVERCALL IS ALSO REVEALING,.

5.   IF YOU RUN YOUR LONG SUIT FIRST. KEEP IN MIND THAT THE PLAYER WITH THE ♡ A WILL HAVE AN EASIER TIME DISCARDING HEARTS THAN THE PLAYER WITH THE ♡ Q.

Section II
DEFENSE

DEVILISH SHIFT (Solution)
(problem on front cover)

North
♠ Q 10 3 2
♡ 4 2
◇ K J 9 8
♣ K J 10

West
♠ A 4
♡ K Q 10 8
◇ A 10 6
♣ 6 5 4 3

East
♠ 9 8 6 5
♡ 9 7 6 3
◇ Q 5 3 2
♣ 2

South
♠ K J 7
♡ A J 5
◇ 7 4
♣ A Q 9 8 7

The ◇ K. Because as you can see West has the ◇ A and East the ◇ Q. Just kidding. The reason you play the ◇ K is that you cannot stand a heart play from East through your A J before the ♠ A is dislodged.

By playing the ◇ K instead of the ◇ J, you increase your chances by 50 percent of keeping East off lead.

If East has the ◇ A, the contract is doomed. Say you play the ◇ J and it drives out the ◇ A. East is certain to return a heart, and now what? If hearts are 4-4 you must lose three hearts along with two aces.

If West started with five hearts along with the ♠ A, he will simply win the ♡ J and return a heart leaving you without resource. If West started with five hearts and does not have the ♠ A, he can win the second heart and shift back to diamonds establishing the setting trick in that suit before spades have been attacked.

As you cannot reasonably make the hand if East has the ◇ A, you must play West for that card and rise with the ◇ K. Even then you are still not out of the woods. You must hope that the opponents cannot cash three diamond tricks once they get in with the ♠ A. As the cards lie, they cannot.

(1) THE WEAK NOTRUMP (1)

North-South vulnerable
Dealer South

North
♠ K 10 2
♡ K Q
♢ Q J 10 9 4 3
♣ 5 4

East (you)
♠ 9 8 4 3
♡ A 6 4
♢ A 7 5
♣ A Q 3

South	West	North	East
*1 NT	Pass	3 NT	Pass
Pass	Pass		

*12-14

Opening lead: ♣ J

1. Which club do you play at trick one?
   You play the ♣ Q which holds.
2. What do you play at trick two?

THE WEAK NOTRUMP (Solution)

North
♠ K 10 2
♡ K Q
◇ Q J 10 9 4 3
♣ 5 4

West
♠ 7 6 5
♡ J 5 3 2
◇ 6 2
♣ J 10 9 7

East
♠ 9 8 4 3
♡ A 6 4
◇ A 7 5
♣ A Q 3

South
♠ A Q J
♡ 10 9 8 7
◇ K 8
♣ K 8 6 2

2. The ace of hearts, (or a low heart).

You have 14 high card points and the dummy has 11 for a total of 25. Declarer must have at least 12, so that leaves partner with a maximum of three high card points. Partner has led the ♣ J, leaving him with at most a queen.

As it is futile to continue with ace and a club (partner cannot have an entry), play partner for the ♡ J instead.

After switching to a heart, you can win the ace of diamonds, cash the ♣ A and continue hearts. If partner has the ♡ J, your defense nets at least five tricks; two clubs, two hearts and a diamond.

KEY LESSON POINTERS

1. ADD YOUR HIGH CARD POINTS TO DUMMY'S HIGH CARD POINTS, THROW IN DECLARER'S AVERAGE COUNT (IN THIS CASE 13), AND SUBTRACT FROM 40 TO GET A BALL PARK FIGURE AS TO PARTNER'S STRENGTH. THEN DEFEND ACCORDINGLY.
2. YOU WERE NOT TOLD WHETHER PARTNER'S LEAD OF THE ♣ J DENIED A HIGHER HONOR, BUT YOU COULD WORK OUT THAT IT DID. IN MORE CASES THAN NOT, "JACK DENIES" IS A USEFUL CONVENTION.

(2) SECOND HAND PLAY

Both sides vulnerable
Dealer South

North
♠ 8 4 3
♡ J 7 6
◇ A 10 7 5
♣ 10 9 4

West (you)
♠ Q 10 9 2
♡ 10 9 8
◇ K 8 6
♣ J 8 6

South	West	North	East
2 ♣ *	Pass	2 ◇ **	Pass
2 ♠	Pass	2 NT	Pass
3 ♠	Pass	4 ◇	Pass
6 ♠	Pass	Pass	Pass

    * Strong and artificial
  ** Waiting

    Opening lead: ♡ 10

    Declarer wins the ♡ A, partner playing the ♡ 2. At trick two declarer cashes the ♠ A and gets the bad news, partner discarding the ♡ 5.
    Undaunted, declarer cashes the ♡ K, partner playing the ♡ 3, and exits with the ◇ 2.
    1. Which diamond do you play? Why?

SECOND HAND PLAY (Solution)

North
♠ 8 4 3
♡ J 7 6
◊ A 10 7 5
♣ 10 9 4

West
♠ Q 10 9 2
♡ 10 9 8
◊ K 8 6
♣ J 8 6

East
♠ —
♡ Q 5 4 3 2
◊ 9 4 3
♣ Q 7 5 3 2

South
♠ A K J 7 6 5
♡ A K
◊ Q J 2
♣ A K

1. The ◊ K! The only way declarer can possibly make this hand is by ruffing twice in his own hand, reducing to your trump length.

   Then, after stripping you of all of your other cards, he can exit with a low trump and force you to lead a trump into his ♠ K J.

   To perform this minor miracle, declarer needs *two* dummy entries. In order to even have the possibility of two dummy entries, declarer needs both the ◊ Q and the ◊ J.

   His plan is to insert the ◊ 10, ruff a heart, cash two clubs and then play a diamond honor. Now it doesn't matter what you do. If you cover, he wins in dummy, ruffs a club, cashes a diamond and exits a low spade endplaying you. If you duck, so does he, crosses to the ◊ A, ruffs a club, and exits a spade. Either way—curtains.

   However, you can frustrate this line of play by inserting the ◊ K at trick four. Now declarer has but one entry to dummy and cannot complete the shortening process.

KEY LESSON POINTERS

1. WHEN THE KEY TO THE DEFENSE IS TO DEPRIVE DECLARER OF AN ADDITIONAL DUMMY ENTRY, SECOND HAND HIGH IS OFTEN AN EFFECTIVE ANSWER.
2. "SURE" TRUMP WINNERS CAN VANISH IN THE NIGHT IF DECLARER CAN MAKE A TRUMP REDUCTION PLAY. HIS PLAN WILL BE TO REDUCE TO YOUR TRUMP LENGTH. YOU CAN SOMETIMES FRUSTRATE HIS EFFORTS BY REFUSING TO FORCE HIM TO RUFF, OR BY KILLING DUMMY ENTRIES THAT HE PLANS TO USE FOR THAT PURPOSE.

(3) IN AGAIN

Both sides vulnerable
Dealer South

North
♠ 10 9 3
♡ Q J
◇ A K 10 9
♣ 6 5 4 3

West (you)
♠ K Q 6
♡ K 7 6
◇ 8 3 2
♣ J 10 9 8

South	West	North	East
1 NT*	Pass	3 NT	Pass
Pass	Pass		

*15-17

Opening lead: ♣ J

Partner plays the ♣ 2 and declarer wins with the ♣ K. At trick two declarer leads the ◇ J to the ◇ K, partner playing the ◇ 6 and leads the ♠ 3. Partner plays the ♠ 4, declarer the ♠ J and you win with the ♠ Q.

You continue with a club, partner follows with the ♣ 7 and declarer wins with the ♣ A.

Once again declarer crosses to a diamond (the ace), partner playing the ◇ 4, and runs the ♡ Q, partner playing the ♡ 2.

1. What do you do now?

IN AGAIN (Solution)

North
♠ 10 9 3
♡ Q J
♢ A K 10 9
♣ 6 5 4 3

West
♠ K Q 6
♡ K 7 6
♢ 8 3 2
♣ J 10 9 8

East
♠ A 8 4 2
♡ 9 8 5 3 2
♢ 6 4
♣ 7 2

South
♠ J 7 5
♡ A 10 4
♢ Q J 7 5
♣ A K Q

1. Win the ♡ K, then play the ♠ K and another spade.

   Declarer is marked with the ♣ A K Q and the ♢ QJxx. (He would not be playing diamonds this way with Jx.)

   That gives declarer a total of seven tricks in the minors. He cannot hold both major aces or else he would have started with 21 high card points!

   Clearly partner has either the ♠ A or the ♡ A. If partner has the ♡ A he needs the ♡ 10 as well for a heart return to work. Furthermore, if declarer had no heart stopper at all he probably would have taken a second spade finesse rather than play a wide open short suit.

   If partner has the ♠ A and declarer the ♡ A, it is necessary to attack spades as declarer now has nine tricks ready to go: seven in the minors along with two hearts.

   The question boils down to: which non-existent suit has declarer attacked, hearts or spades? It looks like spades.

KEY LESSON POINTERS

1. KEEP TRACK OF DECLARER'S HIGH CARD POINTS DURING THE PLAY.
2. KEEP TRACK OF DECLARER'S TRICKS DURING THE PLAY.
3. SNEAKY DECLARERS HAVE BEEN KNOWN TO ATTACK WEAK SUITS AT NO TRUMP TO THROW THE DEFENDERS OFF THE SCENT. NOT MANY DECLARERS ARE BRAVE ENOUGH TO TRY THAT PLOY. THIS ONE WAS.

(4) FINDING A DISCARD

Neither side vulnerable
Dealer South

North
♠ J 10 9
♡ 9 4 3 2
◇ J 9 7
♣ A K J

West (you)
♠ A 8 4 3 2
♡ Q
◇ K 10 4
♣ 5 4 3 2

South	West	North	East
1 NT	Pass	3 NT	Pass
Pass	Pass		

Opening lead: ♠ 3

Partner wins the ♠ K and returns the ♠ 7. When declarer plays the ♠ Q at trick two you decide, right or wrong, to duck the trick.

Declarer continues with the ace-king of hearts, partner playing the ♡ 5 under the ♡ A. What do you discard on the ♡ K?

FINDING A DISCARD (Solution)

North
♠ J 10 9
♡ 9 4 3 2
◇ J 9 7
♣ A K J

West
♠ A 8 4 3 2
♡ Q
◇ K 10 4
♣ 5 4 3 2

East
♠ K 7 5
♡ J 8 7 6 5
◇ 8 6 2
♣ 7 6

South
♠ Q 6
♡ A K 10
◇ A Q 5 3
♣ Q 10 9 8

A diamond. There is a danger that you will be thrown in with a spade and, perhaps, be forced to lead away from your ◇ K.

In order to avoid that ignominy, hang on to all of your clubs. If you don't, declarer can cash three clubs ending in dummy and exit a spade. After cashing three spade winners you will have to lead a diamond.

However, if you discard a diamond, rather than a club at trick four, declarer cannot remove all of your clubs ending in dummy and throw you in with a spade.

If declarer had a third spade in his hand instead of a small diamond, no discard could save you. Declarer could cash *four* rounds of clubs before exiting with a spade.

KEY LESSON POINTERS

I. IF THERE IS A CHANCE THAT YOU MAY BE THROWN IN TO LEAD AWAY FROM A CRITICAL HONOR, EITHER BLANK THE HONOR WITHOUT SWEATING OR KEEP SAFE EXIT CARDS IN ANOTHER SUIT.

(5) AND NOW?

East-West vulnerable
Dealer South

North
♠ 9 8 7
♡ J 2
◇ K Q 3
♣ A J 7 5 4

West (you)
♠ K 6 3
♡ 8 4 3
◇ 10 2
♣ K 9 8 6 2

South	West	North	East
1 ◇	Pass	2 ♣	Pass
2 ◇	Pass	3 ◇	Pass
3 ♡	Pass	4 ◇	Pass
5 ◇	Pass	Pass	Pass

Opening lead: ♠ 3

Partner's jack fetches declarer's ace. Declarer continues with the ♡ A K and ruffs a heart low in dummy, partner following with the ♡ 6, ♡ 9 and ♡ 10.

Declarer cashes the ♣ A and ruffs a club. In his hand at trick seven he produces the ♡ 7. What do you play?

AND NOW? (Solution)

North
♠ 9 8 7
♡ J 2
◇ K Q 3
♣ A J 7 5 4

<table>
<tr><td>

West
♠ K 6 3
♡ 8 4 3
◇ 10 2
♣ K 9 8 6 2

</td><td>

East
♠ Q J 5 4 2
♡ Q 10 9 6
◇ A 4
♣ Q 10

</td></tr>
</table>

South
♠ A 10
♡ A K 7 5
◇ J 9 8 7 6 5
♣ 3

Discard the ♠ K! Declarer should be 2-4-6-1. With 3-4-5-1 he probably would have rebid 3 NT over 3 ◇ . (Or opened 1 ♡ .)

Once it is conceded that 2-4-6-1 is declarer's most likely distribution, the assumption must be made that partner, not declarer, has the trump ace.

If so, you can promote your ◇ 10 to the setting trick by discarding the ♠ K. If declarer leads a diamond from dummy at trick eight, your partner wins, cashes the ♠ Q (declarer is known to have the ♠ 10) and continues a third spade. Declarer is helpless.

KEY LESSON POINTERS

1. WHEN PARTNER PLAYS THIRD HAND HIGH AT TRICK ONE, HE DENIES THE CARD DIRECTLY BENEATH THE ONE HE HAS PLAYED.
2. WHEN LOOKING FOR A TRUMP PROMOTION, IT MIGHT BE NECESSARY TO UNBLOCK FROM A REMAINING DOUBLETON HONOR.
3. THE BETTER YOUR OPPOSITION, THE EASIER TO TRUST THEIR BID-DING. THE WORSE THEY BID, THE WORSE THEY CAN MAKE YOU LOOK ON DEFENSE.
4. IF YOU MUST PROJECT A HIGH TRUMP HONOR IN PARTNER'S HAND TO DEFEAT THE CONTRACT—PROJECT!

(6) LUCKY SPADES

North-South vulnerable
Dealer West

North
♠ A Q 10
♡ Q J 4 3
◇ 7 5 2
♣ A 3 2

East (you)
♠ 9 8 7 6 5
♡ 5 2
◇ 9 8 3
♣ K J 5

West	North	East	South
1 ◇	Dbl.	Pass	4 ♡
Pass	Pass	Pass	

Opening lead: ◇ K

Partner continues with the ◇ A and ◇ J, declarer ruffing the third round, having started with queen doubleton.

At trick four a spade is led to the king and ace and two rounds of trumps are drawn. Declarer continues with a spade to the jack and queen, cashes the ♠ 10, partner discarding a diamond, and leads a low club from dummy.

1. What is declarer's distribution?
2. Which club do you play?

LUCKY SPADES (Solution)

North

♠ A Q 10
♡ Q J 4 3
◇ 7 5 2
♣ A 3 2

West

♠ K J
♡ 7 6
◇ A K J 10 4
♣ 10 7 6 4

East

♠ 9 8 7 6 5
♡ 5 2
◇ 9 8 3
♣ K J 5

South

♠ 4 3 2
♡ A K 10 9 8
◇ Q 6
♣ Q 9 8

1. 3-5-2-3. You do have a complete count, after all.
2. Do not play the ♣ K! You need two club tricks to defeat the contract. If partner has the ♣ Q, it doesn't matter which club you play, so assume declarer has it.

   If declarer has the ♣ Q, he may decide to play your partner for the ♣ K and duck the club lead into partner's hand. Let him try for that pretty endplay.

   Another possibility is to play the ♣ J. If declarer has ♣ Q9x, he may decide that you have both the jack and the ten and duck the trick. If he does, continue with a low club, hoping he plays the ♣ 9. What a con artist you are.

KEY LESSON POINTERS

1. IF YOU CAN'T DEFEAT THE CONTRACT BY HONEST MEANS, TRY A SWINDLE. ALL'S FAIR IN LOVE, WAR AND CARD COMBINATIONS.
2. WHEN SITTING WITH A KING LOCATED BEHIND AN ACE, DON'T AUTO-MATICALLY FLY WITH YOUR KING IF A LOW CARD IS LED FROM THE ACE. UNLESS THE KING IS THE SETTING TRICK, IT IS USUALLY RIGHT TO PLAY LOW AND HOPE PARTNER HAS EITHER THE QUEEN OR THE JACK. KEEP IN MIND THAT IF DECLARER HAD BOTH THE QUEEN AND THE JACK, HE PROBABLY WOULD HAVE LED AN HONOR TOWARDS THE ACE RATHER THAN LEAD LOW FROM THE ACE.

(7) GOOD START (1) (2) (3)

Both sides vulnerable
Dealer South

North
♠ K J 9 5
♡ Q 2
◊ K Q 9 2
♣ 10 7 4

West (you)
♠ A 8
♡ 10 7 5 3
◊ 7 6
♣ K J 5 3 2

South	West	North	East
1 ♡	Pass	1 ♠	Pass
2 ◊	Pass	3 ◊	Pass
3 ♡	Pass	4 ♡	Pass
Pass	Pass		

Opening lead: ♣ 3

You strike gold when partner wins the ♣ A and returns the ♣ 9, declarer playing the ♣ 8 and ♣ Q.
  1. After winning the ♣ K, what do you play at trick three? Why?
       You continue with the ♣ J attempting to shorten declarer's trump length. Declarer ruffs with the ♡ 8.
  2. What are declarer's most likely distributions?
       2-5-4-2 or 1-6-4-2.
  3. At trick three declarer leads the ♠ 3. Which spade do you play?
       The ace.
  4. Partner plays the ♠ 2. What do you play at trick five? Why?

GOOD START (Solution)

North
♠ K J 9 5
♡ Q 2
◇ K Q 9 2
♣ 10 7 4

West	East
♠ A 8	♠ 10 7 6 4 2
♡ 10 7 5 3	♡ 6 4
◇ 7 6	◇ 8 5 4
♣ K J 5 3 2	♣ A 9 6

South
♠ Q 3
♡ A K J 9 8
◇ A J 10 3
♣ Q 8

4. A club—because you want to defeat the contract. Consider the various distributions declarer may have.

   If declarer is 1-6-4-2, you may have the hand beat off the top if partner has a singleton heart honor. If you duck, you lose your spade ace as well as the contract.

   Anytime declarer has five hearts you have an automatic set by winning the ♠ A and returning a club. If declarer ruffs with the ♡ Q in dummy, your ♡ 10 promotes to the setting trick. If he ruffs in his own hand, you will have more trumps than declarer and the hand will become unmanageable.

KEY LESSON POINTERS

1. WHEN HOLDING FOUR TRUMPS IT IS USUALLY RIGHT TO LEAD FROM YOUR LONGEST, RATHER THAN YOUR SHORTEST SIDE SUIT.
2. WHEN DECLARER BIDS TWO SUITS, RECEIVES NO SUPPORT FOR EITHER SUIT AND THEN REBIDS HIS FIRST SUIT, ASSUME 6-4 DISTRIBUTION.
3. WHEN DECLARER BIDS TWO SUITS, RECEIVES SUPPORT FOR HIS SECOND SUIT AND THEN REBIDS HIS FIRST SUIT, ASSUME A SIX CARD SUIT OR A POWERFUL FIVE CARD SUIT.
4. WHEN IT IS OBVIOUS THAT THERE ARE NO TRICKS AVAILABLE IN THE SIDE SUITS, A RUFF AND A SLUFF IS USUALLY THE BEST DEFENSE.

(8) MEASLY PART-SCORE (1)

East-West vulnerable
Dealer East

North
♠ K 10 3
♡ Q 9 8
◇ Q 7 6
♣ Q J 9 4

East (you)
♠ Q 8 4
♡ A 4 3
◇ K J 10 9 5
♣ A 2

East	South	West	North
1 ◇	1 ♡	Pass	2 ♡
Pass	Pass	Pass	

Opening lead: ◇ A

1. West continues with the ◇ 2 which you win. Now what?
   You shift to the ace and a club which declarer wins in his hand with the ♣ K.
2. Declarer now plays the ♠ A and ♠ 9 to the ♠ K, partner playing the ♠ 2 and ♠ 5. How do you play your spades? Why?

MEASLY PART-SCORE (Solution)

North
♠ K 10 3
♡ Q 9 8
◇ Q 7 6
♣ Q J 9 4

West
♠ J 7 6 5 2
♡ 5 2
◇ A 2
♣ 8 7 6 3

East
♠ Q 8 4
♡ A 4 3
◇ K J 10 9 5
♣ A 2

South
♠ A 9
♡ K J 10 7 6
◇ 8 4 3
♣ K 10 5

The ♠ 4 and the ♠ Q. Your plan is to win the first trump, lead a *low* diamond for partner to ruff and ruff his club return. Alas, declarer also knows what you are planning and is trying to counter your brilliant defense.

Declarer is trying to discard a diamond on the third spade hoping you, rather than your partner, win the trick. If so, you will not be able to get your partner in for your cherished club ruff.

In order to counter this diabolical scheme, you must unblock your ♠ Q under the ♠ K. Now, partner, instead of you, has the high spade and declarer's countermeasures won't succeed.

KEY LESSON POINTERS

1. WHEN YOU HOLD THE TRUMP ACE, A SHORT SIDE SUIT, PLUS A PARTNER WHO CAN RUFF SOMETHING, IT IS USUALLY BEST TO VOID YOURSELF BEFORE GIVING PARTNER A RUFF. IF YOU DO, YOU MAY BE ABLE TO GET A RUFF IN RETURN.
2. UNBLOCKING A HIGH HONOR IS ONE WAY TO PROMOTE AN ENTRY TO PARTNER'S HAND. IT MAY ALSO BE A WAY OF FOILING A DECLARER WHO IS TRYING TO PUT YOU ON LEAD. IT MAY ALSO BE A WAY OF LOSING YOUR PARTNER IF IT DOESN'T WORK.

(9) COUNTERMEASURES (1)

East-West vulnerable
Dealer North

North

♠ Q
♡ A K J 7 3
◊ K Q 8 6
♣ K 9 5

East (you)

♠ J 4 2
♡ Q 10 9 5
◊ A 7 5 4
♣ 8 2

North	East	South	West
1 ♡	Pass	1 ♠	Pass
2 NT	Pass	4 ♠	Pass
Pass	Pass		

Opening lead: ◊ J

Declarer covers and you win.
1. What do you return at trick two?
   You return the ♣ 8, declarer plays the ♣ 10 and partner the ♣ A. Partner returns the ♣ 4, dummy plays the ♣ 9 and declarer the ♣ 3. Declarer cashes the ♡ A K, discarding the ♣ Q on the second heart and leads the ♣ K from dummy.
2. What now?

COUNTERMEASURES (Solution)

North
♠ Q
♡ A K J 7 3
◇ K Q 8 6
♣ K 9 5

West
♠ K 3
♡ 8 6 2
◇ J 10 9
♣ A J 7 6 4

East
♠ J 4 2
♡ Q 10 9 5
◇ A 7 5 4
♣ 8 2

South
♠ A 10 9 8 7 6 5
♡ 4
◇ 3 2
♣ Q 10 3

2. Don't ruff! What do you think is going on? Declarer certainly doesn't have both the ace and king of spades. If he did, he would have drawn trumps eons ago.

   Once you realize that partner has a high trump honor, you should be able to visualize two trump tricks—if you don't ruff.

   Besides, what do you think declarer will discard on the ♣ K, a grape?

KEY LESSON POINTERS

1. WHEN IT BECOMES CLEAR THAT DECLARER IS TRYING TO TEMPT YOU TO TRUMP A WINNER WHEN HE HAS NO LOSERS TO DISCARD—DON'T TRUMP—REGARDLESS OF YOUR TRUMP HOLDING! EVEN IF YOU HAVE WORTHLESS TRUMPS IT IS WRONG! DECLARER MAY THEN BE ABLE TO PLACE YOUR PARTNER WITH THE MISSING TRUMP HONORS.
2. WHEN DECLARER FAILS TO DRAW TRUMPS BEFORE DISCARDING LOSERS, CHANCES ARE HE IS MISSING A HIGH TRUMP HONOR—OR TWO.

(10) TRUMP MANAGEMENT (1) (2)

Neither side vulnerable
Dealer South

North
♠ 9 7 6
♡ 10 7 6
◇ J 10 8
♣ A K 7 5

West (you)
♠ 8 5
♡ Q 9 4 2
◇ A K 9 2
♣ Q 10 8

South	West	North	East
1 ♡	Pass	2 ♡	Pass
2 ♠	Pass	3 ♣	Pass
4 ♡	Pass	Pass	Pass

Opening lead: ◇ K

You continue with the ace and a diamond, declarer ruffing the third round.

At trick four declarer plays the ♡ A, partner playing the ♡ J, and continues with a low heart.

1. Which heart do you play?
   You ignore this insulting question and win the ♡ Q, partner discarding a diamond.
2. What do you play now?
   You play a fourth diamond which declarer ruffs in his hand while discarding a spade from dummy. Partner discards the ♣ 6.
3. Declarer continues with the ♠ A K J. What do you play on the third spade? You remain with the ♡ 9 4 and the ♣ Q 10 8; dummy has the ♡ 10 and ♣ A K 7 5.

TRUMP MANAGEMENT (Solution)

North
♠ 9 7 6
♡ 10 7 6
♢ J 10 8
♣ A K 7 5

West	East
West	**East**
♠ 8 5	♠ 10 4 3 2
♡ Q 9 4 2	♡ J
♢ A K 9 2	♢ Q 7 6 5
♣ Q 10 8	♣ 6 4 3 2

South
♠ A K Q J
♡ A K 8 5 3
♢ 4 3
♣ J 9

3. Ruff the ♠ J and insure a one trick set. The best declarer can do is overruff in dummy. Now what? All he can do is play A K and a club which he must ruff. You take the last trick with your low trump.

   By ruffing the ♠ J you insure a one trick set regardless of who has the ♠ Q because declarer cannot get off dummy safely, and you know it.

   If you fail to ruff, declarer discards a club, cashes the ♣ A K and crossruffs the last two tricks.

KEY LESSON POINTERS

1. GIVING DECLARER A RUFF AND A SLUFF TO ENHANCE ONE'S OWN TRUMP HOLDING IS OFTEN AN EFFECTIVE STRATAGEM.
2. VISUALIZING THE POSITION AFTER DECLARER WILL BE LOCKED IN DUMMY IS THE HALLMARK OF AN EXPERT DEFENDER.
3. COUNT TRUMPS!

(11) ZEE STRIP

East-West vulnerable
Dealer East

North
♠ J 4 3 2
♡ K Q 5
◊ A
♣ 9 5 4 3 2

East (you)
♠ Q 9 7
♡ 9 2
◊ K Q J 9 6 3 2
♣ 6

East	South	West	North
3 ◊	4 ♣	4 ◊	5 ♣
Pass	Pass	Pass	

Opening lead: ◊ 4

At trick two declarer plays a club to the ace felling partner's king, continues with three rounds of hearts ending in dummy, partner playing up the line, and leads a low spade.
1. What is declarer's distribution?
2. Which spade do you play? Why?

ZEE STRIP (Solution)

North
♠ J 4 3 2
♡ K Q 5
◇ A
♣ 9 5 4 3 2

West
♠ A 10 8
♡ 10 8 7 4 3
◇ 10 8 7 4
♣ K

East
♠ Q 9 7
♡ 9 2
◇ K Q J 9 6 3 2
♣ 6

South
♠ K 6 5
♡ A J 6
◇ 5
♣ A Q J 10 8 7

1. 3-3-1-6. Declarer would have ruffed any diamond loser in dummy before leading spades, and no partner of yours would play the ♣ K from the ♣ K Q.
2. The ♠ 9. If declarer has the ♠ A there is no defense so assume partner has it. The two critical spade holdings in declarer's hand are K 6 5 and K8x.

   In both cases you must play the ♠ 9 to retain a chance. If you play the ♠ 7, declarer with K 6 5 will play low, knowing your partner must win the trick. With K8x, declarer will insert the ♠ 8, once again endplaying your partner.

   However, if you play the ♠ 9, declarer must guess what to do. If he guesses to play the ♠ K from K 6 5 he is doomed. If he plays low, he will have to guess what to do on the next trick when you lead a low spade.

   Holding K 8x declarer will also have to make the right guesses to land his contract.

KEY LESSON POINTERS

1. WHEN DECLARER IS STRIPPING A HAND AND DOES NOT TAKE ANY RUFFS IN DUMMY'S SHORT SUIT, ASSUME HE HAS NO CARDS TO RUFF. HE PROBABLY HAS THE SAME LENGTH AS DUMMY.
2. WHEN FOLLOWING SUIT IN TRUMPS, DO NOT MISLEAD YOUR PARTNER. WITH QJx PLAY LOW, JACK, NOT LOW, QUEEN. WITH K Q DOUBLETON, PLAY THE QUEEN UNDER THE ACE, NOT THE KING. IF YOU PLAY THE HIGHER EQUAL FIRST, PARTNER WILL MISCOUNT THE HAND. OF COURSE. IF PARTNER DOESN'T COUNT IT DOESN'T MATTER WHICH HONOR YOU PLAY FIRST.
3. IN THE END GAME, AFTER DECLARER HAS STRIPPED THE HAND, SECOND HAND MUST BE CAREFUL NOT TO ALLOW DECLARER TO DUCK A TRICK INTO PARTNER'S HAND—IF PARTNER MAY HAVE A CRITICAL HONOR THAT HE CANNOT AFFORD TO LEAD AWAY FROM.

(12) BIG GAME

Both sides vulnerable
Dealer South

North
♠ A Q 6 4
♡ A Q 3
◇ A 5 4 3 2
♣ K

East (you)
♠ 10 3
♡ J 10 6
◇ J 10 9 8
♣ A 6 5 4

South	West	North	East
1 ♣	Pass	1 ◇	Pass
1 ♡	Pass	1 ♠	Pass
1 NT	Pass	6 NT	Pass
Pass	Pass		

Opening lead: ♣ J

Plan your defense.

BIG GAME (Solution)

North
♠ A Q 6 4
♡ A Q 3
◊ A 5 4 3 2
♣ K

West
♠ J 9 5 2
♡ 8 7 5
◊ 7 6
♣ J 10 9 7

East
♠ 10 3
♡ J 10 6
◊ J 10 9 8
♣ A 6 5 4

South
♠ K 8 7
♡ K 9 4 2
◊ K Q
♣ Q 8 3 2

Duck the trick! For his vulnerable first seat opening bid, South must have the missing kings and queens giving him a bare 13 high card points. (No aces.)

If so, South starts with three spade tricks, four heart tricks, three diamonds and one club for a total of eleven tricks. If you win this trick, partner is sure to be squeezed in the black suits on the run of the red suits.

By refusing this trick, you do not allow declarer to rectify the count (give up a trick) to set the stage for a squeeze.

When this hand came up at the third annual Epson Bridge Tournament in Tokyo (Aug. 85), not one East defender found this defense. Feel better?

KEY LESSON POINTERS

1. WHEN DEFENDING A SMALL SLAM CONTRACT WHERE YOU CAN SEE 11 SURE TRICKS FOR THE DECLARER YOU CAN SOMETIMES GET EITHER YOURSELF OR YOUR PARTNER OFF A SQUEEZE BY REFUSING A TRICK.
2. WHEN A RATIONAL OPPONENT OPENS AN ACELESS WONDER FIRST SEAT VULNERABLE AND SHOWS A BALANCED HAND, ASSUME 13 HIGH CARD POINTS, MINIMUM.

(13) YOUR SHOT

East-West vulnerable
Dealer South

North
♠ A K 3 2
♡ 2
♢ K Q J 9 6 4
♣ 10 5

East (you)
♠ Q J 9 8 5
♡ A 5
♢ 5 3 2
♣ A 6 4

South	West	North	East
1 ♡	Pass	2 ♢	Pass
2 ♡	Pass	2 ♠	Pass
4 ♡	Pass	Pass	Pass

Opening lead: ♣ 3

You rise with the ♣ A and declarer plays the ♣ 2.
1. What is declarer's most likely distribution?
2. What is your plan?

YOUR SHOT (Solution)

North
♠ A K 3 2
♡ 2
◇ K Q J 9 6 4
♣ 10 5

West
♠ 10 7 6
♡ 9 4 3
◇ A 8 7
♣ Q 9 7 3

East (you)
♠ Q J 9 8 5
♡ A 5
◇ 5 3 2
♣ A 6 4

South
♠ 4
♡ K Q J 10 8 7 6
◇ 10
♣ K J 8 2

1. 1-7-1-4. Declarer has shown six or, more likely, seven hearts, and partner's lead appears to be from a four card suit giving declarer four as well. You cannot be completely sure of how the remaining two or three cards are divided.
2. Your best bet is to cash the ♡ A and lead a club. This defense leads to an immediate defeat if partner has the ♣ K J. In fact, you beat the hand two tricks as partner gives you a fourth round club ruff.

   This defense also works if partner has the ♣ Q 9 xx and the ◇ A, the actual case. If declarer ducks your club return, partner wins and cashes the ◇ A for down one. If declarer rises with the ♣ K, twist and turn as he might, he cannot avoid four losers.

   If you switch to a spade, for example, declarer can ruff a club in dummy and come up with ten tricks. Also, if you shift to a low heart, declarer can discard a diamond on a spade winner and later concede *one* club after driving out the ♡ A.

KEY LESSON POINTERS

1. TRY TO WORK OUT DECLARER'S DISTRIBUTION FROM THE BIDDING AND THE OPENING LEAD—BEFORE YOU MAKE ANY DEFENSIVE PLAYS.
2. PROJECT THE MINIMUM AMOUNT OF HONOR STRENGTH NECESSARY IN PARTNER'S HAND CONSISTENT WITH THE BIDDING TO DEFEAT THE CONTRACT, AND PLAY FOR IT.

(14) WHAT'S UP, DOC?

Neither side vulnerable
Dealer West

North
♠ 8 5 2
♡ A K 7 6
◇ Q 4 2
♣ 9 4 3

East (you)
♠ 9 4 3
♡ Q J 10
◇ K 10 6
♣ A K 6 5

West	North	East	South
Pass	Pass	1 ♣	4 ♠
Pass	Pass	Pass	

Opening lead: ♣ 2

You cash two clubs and play a third to declarer's queen, partner following with the ♣ 8 and ♣ 10.

At trick four declarer cashes the ♠ A, partner shedding the ♡ 5. At trick five declarer plays the ♠ 7, partner discards the ♡ 2 and declarer plays the ♠ 5 from dummy.

What is going on, and what do you do?

WHAT'S UP, DOC? (Solution)

North
♠ 8 5 2
♡ A K 7 6
♢ Q 4 2
♣ 9 4 3

West
♠ —
♡ 9 8 5 4 3 2
♢ J 9 8 7
♣ 10 8 2

East
♠ 9 4 3
♡ Q J 10
♢ K 10 6
♣ A K 6 5

South
♠ A K Q J 10 7 6
♡ —
♢ A 5 3
♣ Q J 7

If declarer wants you to win this trick so badly he must be void in hearts and is trying to create a dummy entry with the ♠ 8.

All you need is to find partner with the ♢ J to defeat this contract legitimately, so do not fall into the trap of taking the trick.

If you duck the spade, declarer loses two diamond tricks; take the spade and he loses none. Furthermore, if declarer had the ♢ J he would not be conceding a trump trick.

KEY LESSON POINTERS

1, BEWARE OF GREEKS BEARING GIFTS. IF YOU GET A CHANCE TO WIN A CHEAP TRICK UNNECESSARILY, AND IN TURN CREATE A DUMMY ENTRY FOR DECLARER, IT IS PROBABLY RIGHT NOT TO TAKE THE TRICK.

2. WHEN DECLARER MAKES AN UNUSUAL PLAY, GIVE THE PLAY A LITTLE THOUGHT. SOMETHING IS GOING ON AND YOU WANT TO KNOW WHAT.

(15) WHAT'S THIS?

Neither side vulnerable
Dealer South

North

♠ Q J 10
♡ K J
♢ K Q 9 4
♣ 9 8 3 2

East (you)

♠ K 6 5
♡ 10 9 5 4 3
♢ A 6 5 2
♣ 10

South	West	North	East
1 ♣	Pass	1 ♢	Pass
1 ♠	Pass	2 NT	Pass
3 ♠	Pass	4 ♠	Pass
Pass	Pass		

Opening lead: ♢ J

Dummy plays low. What do you make of all this, and which diamond do you play at trick one? How do you see the defense developing?

WHAT'S THIS? (Solution)

North
♠ Q J 10
♡ K J
♢ K Q 9 4
♣ 9 8 3 2

West
♠ 3 2
♡ A 8 7 6
♢ J 10 8 7
♣ K 7 6

East
♠ K 6 5
♡ 10 9 5 4 3
♢ A 6 5 2
♣ 10

South
♠ A 9 8 7 4
♡ Q 2
♢ 3
♣ A Q J 5 4

Win the ♢ A and shift to a club. Partner's failure to lead the unbid suit suggests the ace of hearts and declarer's play at trick one suggests a singleton diamond plus a distaste for a possible club shift from your side.

Due to the spade position, you must find your partner with the ace or king of clubs in order to get a ruff before declarer can remove trumps. Therefore, you must shift to a club immediately.

With no easy entry to dummy, the best declarer can do is rise with the ♣ A and lead a heart in an effort to get to dummy to take the spade finesse.

This line doesn't work because partner, not you, has the ♡ A. Partner wins the ♡ A, cashes the ♣ K and gives you a club ruff. Down one. You are terrific.

KEY LESSON POINTERS

1. WHEN PARTNER DOES NOT LEAD THE UNBID SUIT VS. A SUIT CONTRACT, THERE IS A GOOD CHANCE HE HAS THE ACE OF THE SUIT AND IS UNWILLING EITHER TO PLUNK IT DOWN OR TO UNDERLEAD IT.
2. WHEN DECLARER MAKES A STRANGE PLAY FROM DUMMY AT TRICK ONE, HE PROBABLY HAS A GOOD REASON. IT IS USUALLY TO BAIT YOU INTO AN ERROR. DON'T DO WHAT HE WANTS YOU TO DO. IN THIS CASE HE WANTS YOU TO PLAY LOW AT TRICK ONE.
3. EVEN THOUGH YOU HAVE A FINESSABLE TRUMP HONOR, DECLARER MAY NOT HAVE AN IMMEDIATE ENTRY TO DUMMY TO TAKE THE FINESSE. YOU MAY STILL HAVE TIME TO ENGINEER A RUFF.
4. A PLAYER WHO OPENS 1 ♣ AND LATER BIDS AND REBIDS SPADES HAS EITHER 5-5 IN THE BLACKS OR SIX CLUBS AND FIVE SPADES.

(16) THE NERVE

Both sides vulnerable
Dealer West

North
♠ 8 4 3
♡ 6
♢ K Q 6 5
♣ K 5 4 3 2

West (you)
♠ K 10 2
♡ 9 3
♢ A J 10 9 8 7
♣ J 10

West	North	East	South
2 ♢ *	Pass	Pass	4 NT
Pass	5 ♣	Pass	6 ♡
Pass	Pass	Pass	

*Weak

Opening lead: ♣ J

Declarer wins the ♣ A, partner playing the ♣ 8, and plays three top hearts, discarding a club and a spade from dummy, partner following with the 4,2, and 10.

At trick five declarer leads a low diamond. Up or down, Mr. Brown?

THE NERVE (Solution)

North
♠ 8 4 3
♡ 6
◇ K Q 6 5
♣ K 5 4 3 2

West
♠ K 10 2
♡ 9 3
◇ A J 10 9 8 7
♣ J 10

East
♠ J 7 6 5
♡ 10 4 2
◇ 4 3
♣ Q 8 7 6

South
♠ A Q 9
♡ A K Q J 8 7 5
◇ 2
♣ A 9

Duck the trick, Mr. Slick. Even though declarer certainly has a singleton diamond, you save a trick by ducking. Win the diamond and declarer gets two diamond tricks; duck the diamond and he only gets one.

You know that declarer has seven trump tricks, two clubs (partner's play of the ♣ 8 has shown the ♣ Q and denied the ♣ 9) plus the ♠ A. If you grab your ace, declarer will have 12 tricks.

However, if you let the diamond ride, Clyde, you have an excellent chance of making two spade tricks, particularly if declarer started with three spades and two clubs.

Declarer may opt to take two spade finesses, first the nine and then the queen. If he does that, you have him beaten. You win the ♠ 10 and exit a club and later make a second spade.

True, declarer can make the hand by ruffing a diamond, playing off his remaining trumps, entering dummy with a club and eventually throwing you in with a diamond, forcing a spade return. However, most declarers are not up to that line of play—besides it loses when the ♠ K is finessable!

KEY LESSON POINTERS

1. WHEN DECLARER LEADS AN OBVIOUS SINGLETON TOWARDS A KQ COMBINATION IT IS USUALLY RIGHT TO DUCK THE TRICK. YES, YOU MAY LOSE YOUR ACE AND YOUR PARTNER, BUT THE TRICK USUALLY COMES BACK WITH INTEREST.
2. WHEN A DEFENDER SIGNALS PARTNER WITH A HIGH SPOT CARD, HE DENIES THE SPOT CARD DIRECTLY ABOVE THE ONE HE HAS PLAYED. EAST'S PLAY OF THE ♣ 8 AT TRICK ONE DENIES THE ♣ 9.

(17) FOUR KINGS IN VIEW

North-South vulnerable
Dealer West

North
♠ K 4
♡ K J 8 7 6
◇ K 10 5
♣ K 10 5

West (you)
♠ 9 8
♡ A Q 5
◇ Q J 9 7 3
♣ Q J 4

West	North	East	South
1 ◇	1 ♡	Pass	4 ♠
Pass	Pass	Pass	

Opening lead: ◇ Q

Declarer plays low from dummy, partner plays the ◇ 8 and declarer the ◇ 2. What do you play now?

FOUR KINGS IN VIEW (Solution)

North
♠ K 4
♡ K J 8 7 6
♢ K 10 5
♣ K 10 5

<table>
<tr><td>

West
♠ 9 8
♡ A Q 5
♢ Q J 9 7 3
♣ Q J 4

</td><td>

East
♠ 7 6
♡ 10 9 4 3
♢ A 8
♣ 9 7 6 3 2

</td></tr>
</table>

South
♠ A Q J 10 5 3 2
♡ 2
♢ 6 4 2
♣ A 8

The ♢ J. Partner knew that you were going to win trick one, so his play was count, not attitude.

Therefore, you know that partner has either ♢ A 8 or ♢ A 8 6 4. With the latter holding he may have supported your suit, so assume the former. Furthermore, you are very unlikely to defeat this contract if declarer started with a singleton diamond. Partner would need the ♣ A to go along with his ♢ A. If he had two bullets he might have bid.

The key to the defense is to tell your partner how to get back to your hand so that he can ruff a third diamond.

By leading the ♢ J, an unnecessarily high card, you announce a reentry in the higher ranking side suit, hearts.

If everything goes according to plan, partner will win the ♢ A, return a heart, ruff your diamond return and give you a nice warm smile.

KEY LESSON POINTERS

1. THIRD HAND GIVES COUNT, NOT ATTITUDE, WHEN THE LOGIC OF THE TRICK MARKS HIS HONOR HOLDING.
2. WHEN LEADING A SUIT THAT PARTNER WILL EITHER RUFF OR WILL WIN AND LATER WISH TO RUFF, LEAD A SUIT PREFERENCE CARD TO INDICATE WHERE YOUR OUTSIDE ENTRY LIES.

(18) GETTING YOUR TWO CENTS WORTH IN (1)

North-South vulnerable
Dealer West

North
♠ A Q 4 3
♡ A Q 7
◇ A Q J 10 2
♣ 8

West (you)
♠ K 10 8
♡ J 4 2
◇ 9
♣ A Q 10 6 5 3

West	North	East	South
Pass	1 ◇	Pass	1 NT
2 ♣	2 ♠	Pass	3 ◇
Pass	3 ♡	Pass	3 NT
Pass	Pass	Pass	

Opening lead: ♣ 6

Partner plays the ♣ 2 and declarer the ♣ 9.

1. How do you read the club position?
    Partner either has a singleton, or, more likely, three small.
2. At trick two declarer emerges with the ♠ J. Do you cover? Why, or why not?

GETTING YOUR TWO CENTS WORTH IN (Solution)

North
♠ A Q 4 3
♡ A Q 7
◇ A Q J 10 2
♣ 8

West	East
♠ K 10 8	♠ 9 7 6
♡ J 4 2	♡ K 8 6 3
◇ 9	◇ 6 4 3
♣ A Q 10 6 5 3	♣ 7 4 2

South
♠ J 5 2
♡ 10 9 5
◇ K 8 7 5
♣ K J 9

2. Do not cover! As far as spades go, it is obviously right to cover in order to promote a later spade trick. However, as far as the hand goes, it is clearly a mistake!

Declarer is marked with the ◇ K from both the bidding and the fact that he did not attack the suit at once. Therefore, covering the ♠ J gives declarer nine tricks; five diamonds, two spades, a heart and a club.

What will happen if you don't cover? Declarer may decide you do not have the ♠ K and rely on the heart finesse instead. Remember, declarer is not looking into your hand and does not know which major suit king you have. And you know from your club holding that he cannot afford to take a losing finesse.

Was he just laying a trap for you? Did you fall in?

KEY LESSON POINTERS

1. AT TRICK ONE, WHEN THIRD HAND CANNOT BEAT DUMMY'S PLAY OF THE QUEEN OR LESS, THIRD HAND GIVES COUNT.
2. WHEN IT IS CLEAR THAT DECLARER HAS TO DECIDE WHICH ONE OF TWO FINESSES TO TAKE TO MAKE HIS CONTRACT, HELP HIM MAKE THE WRONG DECISION. ONE WAY IS NOT TO COVER AN HONOR WITH AN HONOR IF HE BEGINS BY ATTACKING THE SUIT IN WHICH THE FINESSE WORKS. HE MAY CHANGE HIS MIND AND FALL BACK ON THE OTHER FINESSE—THE LOSING ONE. HOW CLEVER YOU ARE.

(19) HOPING FOR THE BEST (1)

East-West vulnerable
Dealer North

North
♠ K Q 3
♡ A 4 3
♢ J 8
♣ Q J 10 9 2

East (you)
♠ 6 5
♡ Q J 5
♢ A 7 6 5 4 2
♣ A 3

North	East	South	West
1 ♣	1 ♢	2 NT	Pass
3 NT	Pass	Pass	Pass

Opening lead: ♢ 9

1. Dummy plays the ♢ J, which diamond do you play?
   You signal with the ♢ 7. Declarer wins the ♢ Q and leads a low club. Partner plays the ♣ K and returns the ♢ 3. You win and play a third diamond, partner discarding the ♣ 7, dummy shedding a club.
   Declarer cashes the ♠ K, partner playing the ♠ 10, and continues with the ♠ Q, partner playing the ♠ 7, and a low spade to the ace as you discard a diamond. Declarer now produces the ♠ J, partner following, discarding another club from dummy.
2. What do you discard on the fourth spade? (You remain with three hearts, two winning diamonds, and the ♣ A.)

HOPING FOR THE BEST (Solution)

North
♠ K Q 3
♡ A 4 3
◇ J 8
♣ Q J 10 9 2

West
♠ 10 9 8 7
♡ 10 8 7 6
◇ 9 3
♣ K 7 4

East
♠ 6 5
♡ Q J 5
◇ A 7 6 5 4 2
♣ A 3

South
♠ A J 4 2
♡ K 9 2
◇ K Q 10
♣ 8 6 5

2. The ♡ 5. Declarer needs the ♡ K to justify his bid and that card brings declarer's trick total to eight. If you discard a diamond, declarer will be able to set up a ninth trick in clubs without having to worry about you cashing the setting tricks in diamonds. (You will only have one left.)

Your only chance is to discard a heart and hope that partner has the ♡ 10. Good partners have those cards. If partner has the ♡ 10, declarer has no place to go for a ninth trick other than clubs. That line won't work because you have the ace along with the setting tricks in diamonds.

KEY LESSON POINTERS

1. WHEN FORCED TO MAKE A CHOICE BETWEEN DISCARDING ESTAB-
LISHED WINNERS OR UNGUARDING A SUIT, UNGUARD THE SUIT IF YOU
WILL NOT HAVE ENOUGH ESTABLISHED WINNERS TO DEFEAT THE
CONTRACT WHEN YOU GAIN THE LEAD. DECLARER MAY NOT KNOW
YOU HAVE UNGUARDED THE SUIT OR PARTNER MAY HAVE A VITAL
CARD IN THE SUIT WHICH WILL PREVENT THE RUN OF THE SUIT.
2. UNGUARDING A QUEEN OR BLANKING A KING ONLY HURTS FOR A
LITTLE WHILE. HOWEVER, SWEAT ON THE BROW, TREMBLING, OR
SOFT MOANS DO GIVE THE SHOW AWAY.

(20) PUSH, PUSH, PUSH

Neither side vulnerable
Dealer East

North
♠ Q 5 3
♡ K
◇ A K Q J 8 3
♣ J 9 5

West (you)
♠ 10 7 6
♡ A 9 8 3 2
◇ 7 6
♣ 7 6 2

East	South	West	North
1 ♣	Pass	1 ♡	2 ◇
2 ♡	2 ♠	Pass	Pass
3 ♡	Pass	Pass	3 ♠
Pass	Pass	Pass	

Opening lead: ♣ 2

East wins the king-ace of clubs, declarer playing the three and the queen. At trick three East shifts to the ♡ 7 to your ace and declarer's six. Now what?

PUSH, PUSH, PUSH (Solution)

North
♠ Q 5 3
♡ K
◇ A K Q J 8 3
♣ J 9 5

West	East
♠ 10 7 6	♠ A 2
♡ A 9 8 3 2	♡ J 7 5 4
◇ 7 6	◇ 9 2
♣ 7 6 2	♣ A K 10 8 4

South
♠ K J 9 8 4
♡ Q 10 6
◇ 10 5 4
♣ Q 3

Play a third club. In order to have any chance to defeat this contract partner must have the ♠ A. If he does, and declarer errs by leading a spade to the king and a spade to the queen, partner can return a fourth club and promote your ♠ 10.

Returning a heart to force dummy and promote your ♠ 10 (if partner has the ♠ K) will not defeat three spades. Furthermore, it is hard to imagine partner, who is marked with four hearts on the bidding, holding the ♡ Q after returning the ♡ 7. Which four hearts can he hold?

No. If partner wanted you to continue hearts, he would have led a low heart. He had to get you to play a third round of clubs, and he did this by leading a high, not a low, heart.

KEY LESSON POINTERS

1. BY PROJECTING A HIGH TRUMP HONOR IN PARTNER'S HAND, YOU MAY BE ABLE TO ENVISION A TRUMP PROMOTION PLAY.
2. AT TIMES THE ONLY WAY TO DEFEAT A CONTRACT IS TO HOPE THAT DECLARER ERRS SLIGHTLY IN THE PLAY. (HE MUST LEAD LOW SPADES TWICE FROM DUMMY.)
3. WHEN PARTNER WANTS YOU TO CONTINUE A SUIT, HE LEADS A LOW SPOT CARD, NOT A HIGH ONE.

(21) NOT WITH CHILDREN (1)

Neither side vulnerable
Dealer North

North
♠ K 4 2
♡ Q 7 4
◇ A K J 10 4
♣ K J

East (you)
♠ A Q 9 8 7 6 5
♡ —
◇ 7 6
♣ 10 9 8 7

North	East	South	West
1 NT	3 ♠	4 ♡	Pass
Pass	Pass		

Opening lead: ♠ 10

Dummy plays low and you win the ♠ Q, declarer playing the ♠ J.
1. What do you play now?
    You try the ♠ A (you probably need two spade tricks to defeat the contract), declarer following, and partner discarding the ♣ 6.
2. Now what?

NOT WITH CHILDREN (Solution)

North
♠ K 4 2
♡ Q 7 4
◇ A K J 10 4
♣ K J

West
♠ 10
♡ J 10 3 2
◇ 9 8
♣ A 6 5 4 3 2

East
♠ A Q 9 8 7 6 5
♡ —
◇ 7 6
♣ 10 9 8 7

South
♠ J 3
♡ A K 9 8 6 5
◇ Q 5 3 2
♣ Q

2. Return a club, not a spade. Your partner has signaled with a high club (there are four lower clubs outstanding). If he had wanted you to continue a spade, he would have discarded a low club. Trust.

   Notice that if you return a spade, declarer discards a club, partner ruffs with his natural trump trick and school is out.

   If you return a club, partner wins the ♣ A and still makes a trump trick. Down one. Better.

KEY LESSON POINTERS

1. EVEN WHEN VOID, PARTNER MAY NOT WANT A RUFF. IF PARTNER SIGNALS ENCOURAGEMENT IN ANOTHER SUIT, LEAD THAT SUIT INSTEAD OF GIVING PARTNER A RUFF.
2. TURNING THE TABLES, WHEN PARTNER CASHES A WINNER IN A SUIT IN WHICH YOU ARE VOID, DO NOT SIGNAL ENCOURAGEMENT IN ANOTHER SUIT, UNLESS YOU WANT THAT SUIT LED. IF YOU WANT A RUFF, DO NOT MAKE ENCOURAGING NOISES IN ANOTHER SUIT. HE MAY BELIEVE YOU.

(22) TELLTALE CARD (1)

East-West vulnerable
Dealer North

North
♠ Q J 9 7 6
♡ A 10 4
◇ A Q 2
♣ K Q

East (you)
♠ K 10 4 3
♡ K 9 3 2
◇ K 8 6
♣ 9 6

North	East	South	West
1 ♠	Pass	1 NT	Pass
3 NT	Pass	Pass	Pass

Opening lead: ◇ J (Denies a higher honor)

Dummy plays the ◇ A and you signal with the ◇ 8.
1. At trick two a low heart is led from dummy. Which heart do you play?
    You rise with the ♡ K, partner playing the ♡ 5, declarer the ♡ 7.
2. Now what?

TELLTALE CARD (Solution)

North
♠ Q J 9 7 6
♡ A 10 4
◇ A Q 2
♣ K Q

West	East
♠ A 2	♠ K 10 4 3
♡ J 8 5	♡ K 9 3 2
◇ J 10 9 5 3	◇ K 8 6
♣ 8 7 5	♣ 9 6

South
♠ 8 5
♡ Q 7 6
◇ 7 4
♣ A J 10 4 3 2

2. Lead a low spade. South is apparently short in diamonds, has fewer than three spades, and did not try to get to his hand to take a heart finesse.

　All this leads one to believe that South has a hidden club suit and is leading toward the ♡ Q for ninth trick.

　You can stop this nonsense by putting partner in with the ♠ A for a diamond lead through the queen. Even if declarer ducks partner's high diamond play, you will have established five tricks for your side; two spades, two diamonds and the ♡ K.

KEY LESSON POINTERS

1. BE WARY OF LONG HIDDEN MINOR SUITS WHEN THE RESPONSE TO A MAJOR SUIT OPENING BID IS ONE NOTRUMP.
2. WHEN A LOW CARD IS LED FROM THE A 10x(x) IN DUMMY, AND YOU HOLD THE K 9x(x) BEHIND DUMMY, DECLARER PROBABLY HAS THE QUEEN AND PARTNER THE JACK.

　IF DECLARER HAD BOTH THE QUEEN AND THE JACK HE WOULD HAVE LED AN HONOR FROM THE CLOSED HAND. FURTHERMORE, BECAUSE YOU HOLD THE NINE DECLARER CANNOT HAVE A GUESS IN THE SUIT IF YOU PLAY LOW.

　IF YOU DID NOT HAVE THE NINE, DECLARER MIGHT HAVE Q 9x(x) AND BE FORCED TO GUESS IF YOU PLAY LOW. THE NINE IN YOUR HAND CLARIFIES THE HEART POSITION.

(23) DIAMOND IN THE ROUGH

East-West vulnerable
Dealer North

North
♠ A 9 8 7
♡ A J
♢ A 8 6 4 2
♣ 7 6

East (you)
♠ Q J 10
♡ Q 4 3
♢ K 10 5 3
♣ 5 4 3

North	East	South	West
1 ♢	Pass	1 ♡	Pass
1 ♠	Pass	3 NT	Pass
Pass	Pass		

Opening lead: ♣ J (Denies a higher honor)

Declarer wins the ♣ Q and leads the ♢ 9 to the ♢ A, partner playing the ♢ Q. At trick three declarer leads a low diamond from dummy which you win with the ♢ K, declarer unblocking the ♢ J. Partner discards the ♠ 4.
What do you play now?

DIAMOND IN THE ROUGH (Solution)

North
♠ A 9 8 7
♡ A J
◊ A 8 6 4 2
♣ 7 6

<table>
<tr><td>West</td><td>East</td></tr>
<tr><td>♠ 6 5 4</td><td>♠ Q J 10</td></tr>
<tr><td>♡ K 10 8 2</td><td>♡ Q 4 3</td></tr>
<tr><td>◊ Q</td><td>◊ K 10 5 3</td></tr>
<tr><td>♣ J 10 9 8 2</td><td>♣ 5 4 3</td></tr>
</table>

South
♠ K 3 2
♡ 9 7 6 5
◊ J 9 7
♣ A K Q

The ♡ 3. Time is of the essence. Count declarer's tricks. You know he has the three top clubs and can set up the diamonds for three more tricks. You are also looking at two major suit aces in the dummy and a declarer who has shown 13-15 high card points in the bidding.

Your only chance is to find a suit where you can build up three tricks before your second diamond stopper is removed.

Obviously, it isn't clubs. What about spades? Even if partner has the ♣ K, you cannot set up three tricks in the suit. (The suit is blocked.)

Besides, partner would not have discarded a spade had he wanted you to lead that suit. He would have made a discouraging heart discard instead. Remember, he knows that you know his club holding.

If you switch to a low heart, partner's king will drive out the ♡ A. When you get in with the ♡ 10, you will cash the ♡ Q and lead a low heart, completing your great triumph.

KEY LESSON POINTERS

1. COUNTING THEIR TRICKS TELLS YOU WHETHER TO PLAY AN ACTIVE OR PASSIVE DEFENSE. ON THIS HAND AN ACTIVE DEFENSE IS CALLED FOR.
2. VS. NO TRUMP PARTNER USUALLY DISCARDS FROM SUITS HE DOES NOT WANT LED, RETAINING LENGTH AND STRENGTH IN SUITS HE DOES WANT LED.
3. DON'T LET THE FACT THAT SOMEONE HAS BID A SUIT PREVENT YOU FROM LEADING IT. IT IS QUITE FASHIONABLE NOWADAYS TO RESPOND TO A MINOR SUIT OPENING WITH FOUR SMALL CARDS.

(24) REAL MEN DON'T GIVE COUNT

Neither side vulnerable
Dealer South

North
♠ 10 2
♡ K Q J 7
◇ 6 5
♣ K 10 9 8 2

West (you)
♠ Q 9 4 3
♡ 9
◇ K 10 8 3 2
♣ Q 5 3

South	West	North	East
1 NT*	Pass	2 ♣	Pass
2 ♠	Pass	3 NT	Pass
Pass	Pass		

*16-18

Opening lead: ◇ 3

Partner plays the ◇ Q and declarer wins the ◇ A. At trick two declarer leads the ♣ 7 to the ♣ K, partner playing the ♣ 4, and at trick three the ♣ 10 to the ♣ J, partner playing the ♣ 6.
After winning the ♣ Q, what do you play?

REAL MEN DON'T GIVE COUNT (Solution)

North
♠ 10 2
♡ K Q J 7
♢ 6 5
♣ K 10 9 8 2

West
♠ Q 9 4 3
♡ 9
♢ K 10 8 3 2
♣ Q 5 3

East
♠ A J 8
♡ 10 8 5 4 3
♢ Q 9 4
♣ 6 4

South
♠ K 7 6 5
♡ A 6 2
♢ A J 7
♣ A J 7

The ♠ 9. The club suit is blocked (partner doesn't have to give count every time declarer plays a suit), which, in turn, indicates that declarer has the ♡ A.

If this assumption is valid, declarer has nine tricks ready to roll; four clubs, four hearts, plus the ♢ A.

Your only problem is to decide whether declarer has ♢ A J blank or ♢ AJx and partner the ♠ A.

If you go back to the bidding you will come to the conclusion that declarer cannot have ♢ A J blank. South is known to hold four spades and three clubs. If he had four hearts and two diamonds, he would either have bid 2 ♡ over 2 ♣ or 4 ♡ over 3 NT, depending upon methods.

Once you conclude that declarer has ♢ AJx, you must shift to a spade. Why the nine? Because you don't want your partner to return a spade, which might be the winning play from his point of view.

KEY LESSON POINTERS

1. GOOD PARTNERS DO NOT GIVE COUNT IN EVERY SUIT ON EVERY HAND. IT GIVES AWAY TOO MUCH INFORMATION.
2. REVIEW THE BIDDING. IT OFTENTIMES REVEALS DECLARER'S EXACT DISTRIBUTION.
3. WHEN YOU LEAD ONE SUIT AND THEN SHIFT TO ANOTHER, PARTNER HAS TO KNOW WHICH SUIT YOU WANT RETURNED. IF YOU WANT THE FIRST SUIT RETURNED, SHIFT TO A HIGH SPOT CARD IN THE SECOND SUIT. IF YOU WANT THE SECOND SUIT RETURNED, SHIFT TO A LOW SPOT CARD.
4. PLAY WITH SOMEBODY WHO KNOWS ALL OF THIS—OR GIVE THEM A COPY OF THIS BOOK.

(25) COVER UP

North-South vulnerable
Dealer South

North

♠ A 3
♡ J 4
◇ K J 10 9 6 2
♣ J 5 4

East (you)

♠ 10 7 6 5 4
♡ Q 5 3
◇ 4 3
♣ A K 8

South	West	North	East
1 ♣	Pass	1 ◇	Pass
1 NT	Pass	3 ◇	Pass
3 NT	Pass	Pass	Pass

Opening lead: ♠ Q

The ♠ A wins the first trick, as you signal encouragement with the ♠ 7. At trick two the ♡ J is led from dummy. Do you cover or not? Why?

COVER UP (Solution)

North
♠ A 3
♡ J 4
◇ K J 10 9 6 2
♣ J 5 4

West	East
♠ Q J 9 8	♠ 10 7 6 5 4
♡ A 8 7 6 2	♡ Q 5 3
◇ 8 5	◇ 4 3
♣ 7 3	♣ A K 8

South
♠ K 2
♡ K 10 9
◇ A Q 7
♣ Q 10 9 6 2

Do not cover! The answer to the question in hearts rests with the diamond suit! The fact that declarer has won the first trick in dummy isolating the suit without an entry makes it clear that the diamonds are solid. If this is the case, declarer has six diamonds and two spades. If he has the ♡ A the hand cannot be defeated, so assume partner has that card.

If partner has the ♡ A, declarer certainly has either ♡ K10x, or, more likely, K 10 9. Cover and you eliminate the guess. Play low smoothly and declarer may play you for the ♡ A and rise with the ♡ K. If he does, down one.

KEY LESSON POINTERS

1. YOU MUST COUNT DECLARER'S TRICKS AS SOON AS THE DUMMY COMES DOWN.
2. IF PARTNER LEADS AN HONOR CARD, YOU CAN USUALLY COUNT DECLARER'S TRICKS IN THAT SUIT.
3. IF DUMMY HAS A LONG STRONG SUIT THAT DECLARER DOES NOT TOUCH, ASSUME HE HAS THE MISSING HONORS IN THE SUIT.
4. IF YOU NEED PARTNER TO HOLD A SPECIFIC CARD TO DEFEAT THE CONTRACT, ASSUME HE HAS IT, AND PLAY ACCORDINGLY.
5. SOMETIMES THE PROPER PLAY IN A SUIT (COVERING THE ♡ J), IS NOT THE PROPER PLAY FOR THE PARTICULAR HAND THAT YOU ARE DEFENDING.

Section III
DEFENSE

(26) NO INSULTS, PLEASE

Both sides vulnerable
Dealer West

North
♠ K Q J 6 3
♡ Q J 10 6 2
♢ 6 2
♣ Q

East (you)
♠ 9
♡ 9 4 3
♢ 5 4 3
♣ A K 9 5 4 3

West	North	East	South
1 ♢	2 ♢ *	3 ♣	4 ♠
5 ♢	Pass	Pass	5 ♠
Dbl.	Pass	Pass	Pass

*Majors

Opening lead: ♡ A (You lead K from AK.)

You play the ♡ 3 and partner shifts to the ♣ 10 which you win with the ♣ K. What do you play now?

NO INSULTS, PLEASE (Solution)

North
♠ K Q J 6 3
♡ Q J 10 6 2
◇ 6 2
♣ Q

<table>
<tr><td>

West
♠ 7 4
♡ A
◇ A Q J 10 9 8 7
♣ 10 6 2

</td><td>

East
♠ 9
♡ 9 4 3
◇ 5 4 3
♣ A K 9 5 4 3

</td></tr>
</table>

South
♠ A 10 8 5 2
♡ K 8 7 5
◇ K
♣ J 8 7

The ♡ 4. Partner must have led a singleton, and your return of a low heart indicates that your remaining high card strength is in the lower ranking suit, clubs.

Holding the ◇ K, you would return your ♡ 9 to show a possible entry in the higher ranking side suit, diamonds.

Once partner knows that you do not have the ◇ K, he will cash the ◇ A after ruffing your heart return and defeat the contract two tricks.

Returning a diamond, rather than a heart, at trick three is an insult to your partner's intelligence.

KEY LESSON POINTERS

1. WHEN BOTH YOU AND YOUR PARTNER HAVE INDICATED STRONG SUITS DURING THE BIDDING AND PARTNER LEADS ONE OF THEIR SUITS, THERE CAN ONLY BE ONE REASON: PARTNER IS LOOKING FOR A RUFF.
2. WHEN RETURNING A SUIT THAT YOU SUSPECT PARTNER WILL RUFF, TELL YOUR PARTNER WHERE YOUR OUTSIDE STRENGTH LIES BY THE SIZE OF THE CARD YOU RETURN.
3. WHEN PARTNER REBIDS A SUIT ALL BY HIS LONESOME AT THE FIVE LEVEL, VULNERABLE, ASSUME A SEVEN CARD SUIT—OR A MADMAN.

(27) THE WEAK TWO

Both sides vulnerable
Dealer East

North
♠ 6 5 2
♡ K J 9
◇ K Q 10 2
♣ A 3 2

East (you)
♠ A J 10 8 4 3
♡ 7 2
◇ A 6
♣ J 10 9

East	South	West	North
2 ♠	Pass	Pass	Dbl.
Pass	3 NT	Pass	Pass
Pass			

Opening lead: ♠ K

Plan your defense. Which spade do you play?

THE WEAK TWO (Solution)

North
♠ 6 5 2
♡ K J 9
◇ K Q 10 2
♣ A 3 2

West
♠ K
♡ 10 6 5 4 3
◇ 8 7 5 3
♣ 7 6 4

East
♠ A J 10 8 4 3
♡ 7 2
◇ A 6
♣ J 10 9

South
♠ Q 9 7
♡ A Q 8
◇ J 9 4
♣ K Q 8 5

All you have to do to get this one right is overtake partner's obvious singleton and continue with the ♠ J (or ♠ 10) to drive out the ♠ Q.

Then you must hope that declarer does not have nine tricks to take outside of the diamond suit.

If you do not overtake, you will not be able to develop your spades.

KEY LESSON POINTERS

1. NEVER SIGNAL ENCOURAGEMENT WHEN YOU CAN AFFORD TO OVER-TAKE.
2. I HAVE TALKED TO FRIENDS WHO HAVE GONE THROUGH MY BOOKS WITHOUT GETTING ONE PROBLEM RIGHT. THIS PROBLEM IS DEDI-CATED TO THEM, JUDY.

(28) ALL IN VIEW (1)

East-West vulnerable
Dealer North

North
♠ 10 7 6
♡ A K J 9 2
◇ K J 4
♣ A Q

East (you)
♠ Q 9 2
♡ 7 6 5 3
◇ Q 9 7
♣ 8 6 5

North	East	South	West
1 ♡	Pass	1 NT	Pass
2 NT	Pass	3 ♣	Pass
3 ◇	Pass	3 NT	Pass
Pass	Pass		

Opening lead: ◇ 3

1. Dummy plays low, which diamond do you play? Why?
   The ◇ Q. Partner should have the ◇ A from his failure to lead a high spade which he would with the A K. Give declarer a spade honor and a likely ♣ K and he can hardly hold the ◇ A as well. Right?
2. You win the trick, declarer playing the ◇ 5. What do you return at trick two?

ALL IN VIEW (Solution)

North
♠ 10 7 6
♡ A K J 9 2
◇ K J 4
♣ A Q

West	East
West	**East**
♠ A J 8 4	♠ Q 9 2
♡ Q 10	♡ 7 6 5 3
◇ A 8 6 3 2	◇ Q 9 7
♣ 10 7	♣ 8 6 5

South
♠ K 5 3
♡ 8 4
◇ 10 5
♣ K J 9 4 3 2

2. The ♠ Q. Declarer is known to have six clubs, probably less than four spades, a likely doubleton diamond in view of partner's lead and, therefore, a doubleton heart.

  If declarer has the ♣ K, the suit runs for six tricks. As the hearts are running for five tricks, you had better run with your tricks!

  You must project a spade holding that will give you a chance for at least three *quick* spade tricks. Declarer's most likely holding is Kxx. (You cannot defeat the contract if declarer has the ♠ A.)

  By leading the ♠ Q you give declarer a problem. If he plays you for the queen and jack, he will play low. If he does, you scoop in four spade tricks. Down two. Notice that you cannot afford to lead a low spade. Declarer will simply duck it around to the ♠ 10 and partner will be helpless.

KEY LESSON POINTERS

1. WHEN PARTNER LEADS LOW AND YOU HAVE Q 9x IN BACK OF K Jx IN THE DUMMY, YOU HAVE A PROBLEM WHEN DUMMY PLAYS LOW. AT A SUIT CONTRACT, WHERE PARTNER WILL NOT BE UNDERLEADING AN ACE, PLAY THE NINE. AT NOTRUMP IT IS NOT AS CLEAR. IF THERE IS A GOOD CHANCE THAT PARTNER HAS THE ACE, OR NEEDS THE ACE TO DEFEAT THE CONTRACT, PLAY THE QUEEN.
2. WHEN THE DECLARER HAS A COMBINED HOLDING OF Kxx FACING 10xx, AND EITHER DEFENDER IS LEADING THROUGH THE KING NEEDING THREE QUICK TRICKS, THE PROPER CARD TO LEAD IS THE JACK FROM Jxx OR THE QUEEN FROM Qxx.

(29) TRICK ONE, AGAIN

East-West vulnerable
Dealer South

North
♠ Q 9 6 3 2
♡ J 10 2
◇ Q 2
♣ A Q 10

East (you)
♠ 10 8 4
♡ 5 4 3
◇ A 7 6
♣ 9 7 5 4

South	West	North	East
1 ♡	Pass	1 ♠	Pass
2 ◇	Pass	3 ♡	Pass
4 ♡	Pass	Pass	Pass

Opening lead: ♠ K

1. Assuming you play attitude signals when the king is led and the queen is in the dummy, which spade do you play? Why?

TRICK ONE, AGAIN (Solution)

North
♠ Q 9 6 3 2
♡ J 10 2
♢ Q 2
♣ A Q 10

West	**East**
♠ A K 5	♠ 10 8 4
♡ K 6	♡ 5 4 3
♢ 9 8 5 4	♢ A 7 6
♣ J 8 3 2	♣ 9 7 5 4

South
♠ J 7
♡ A Q 9 8 7
♢ K J 10 3
♣ K 6

1. The ♠ 8. When you play attitude signals, you normally play a high card when you want the suit continued and low when you don't.

   However, there are other factors. When you play low, your partner assumes you can stand the logical shift. In this case the logical shift is to a club and you can't stand it.

   If declarer is 2-5-4-2 and partner shifts to a club, you will lose your second spade trick. Therefore, you should give your partner a false signal.

   Even if declarer ruffs the second spade you have lost nothing. You have no club tricks coming anyway, and one or two diamond discards will do declarer no good.

   If partner continues with the ♠ A, play the ♠ 10. Partners versed in false signals will understand what you have done and why. Even if partner mistakenly shifts to a club after cashing both spades, he will have another chance to shift to a diamond upon winning the ♡ K.

KEY LESSON POINTERS

1. DON'T GO OUT OF YOUR WAY TO GIVE PARTNER A FALSE COME-ON SIGNAL WHEN HE LEADS THE KING AND THE QUEEN IS IN THE DUMMY. ONLY DO IT WHEN YOU FEAR HIS ACE WILL BE LOST IF HE MAKES THE LOGICAL SHIFT AT TRICK TWO.
2. SOME PLAYERS GIVE ATTITUDE WHEN THE KING IS LED AND DUMMY HAS THE QUEEN, OTHERS GIVE COUNT. A REASONABLE COMPROMISE IS TO GIVE ATTITUDE UNLESS:
   (1) THIRD HAND HAS SUPPORTED THE SUIT.
   (2) THE CONTRACT IS AT THE FIVE LEVEL OR HIGHER.
   (3) DECLARER HAS BID TWO OTHER SUITS.

(30) TAKING ADVANTAGE OF THE VULNERABILITY (1)

North-South vulnerable
Dealer West

North
♠ Q 9 4 3
♡ A Q 4
◇ 2
♣ A K J 4 3

               East (you)
               ♠ J 8 7 6
               ♡ 5
               ◇ A J 10 9 8 7
               ♣ 8 7

West	North	East	South
Pass	1 ♣	3 ◇	3 ♡
Pass	4 ◇	Pass	4 NT
Pass	5 ♡	Pass	6 NT
Pass	Pass	Pass	

Opening lead: ◇ 3

1. Which diamond do you play at trick one?
   As declarer is marked with the ◇ K and probably the ◇ K Q, play the ◇ 7.
   Declarer wins the ◇ K and races off five rounds of hearts discarding two clubs from dummy. Partner discards the ◇ 5 on the fifth heart.
2. What four discards do you rnake?

TAKING ADVANTAGE OF THE VULNERABILITY
(Solution)

North
♠ Q 9 4 3
♡ A Q 4
◇ 2
♣ A K J 4 3

West
♠ 10 2
♡ 10 9 3 2
◇ 5 4 3
♣ Q 10 9 6

East
♠ J876
♡ 5
◇ A J 10 9 8 7
♣ 8 7

South
♠ A K 5
♡ K J 8 7 6
◇ K Q 6 3
♣ 5 2

2. Three diamonds and a club, clutching those four spades for dear life.
    Declarer can still make the hand, but in real life an expert found a way to go down.

KEY LESSON POINTERS

1. VS. NO TRUMP WHEN THE DUMMY HAS A SINGLETON AND BIDDING AND/OR LEAD HAS INDICATED THAT THE DECLARER HAS THE K Qx (OR AT LEAST THE KING), IN BACK OF YOUR A J 10 COMBINATION, IT IS USUALLY RIGHT FOR THIRD HAND NOT TO PLAY THE ACE. THE SUIT CANNOT BE LED A SECOND TIME FROM DUMMY AND DECLARER WINDS UP WITH ONE TRICK INSTEAD OF TWO.
2. WHEN DISCARDING, KEEP LENGTH PARITY WITH THE DUMMY. (DUMMY HAS FOUR SPADES--YOU KEEP FOUR SPADES.)ALSO, DO NOT DISCARD DOWN TO A VOID. FOR EXAMPLE, IF YOU WERE TO DISCARD BOTH CLUBS, DECLARER COULD TEST CLUBS BY PLAYING THE ACE. WHEN DECLARER SEES YOU SHOW OUT, IT IS NOT TOO DIFFICULT FOR HIM TO FINESSE PARTNER'S QUEEN. THIS TYPE OF DISCARDING HAS A WAY OF UPSETTING PARTNER.
3. YES, 6 ♡ WOULD HAVE BEEN A SAFER CONTRACT.
4. VS. NT LEAD LOW FROM THREE (OR FOUR) SMALL IN PARTNER'S SUIT IF YOU HAVE NOT SUPPORTED; HIGHEST IF YOU HAVE.

(31) NO STAYMAN?

Both sides vulnerable
Dealer South

North
♠ Q 10 7
♡ J 10 7 2
◇ K Q J 3
♣ Q 10

East (you)
♠ A J 6 2
♡ A 6 5
◇ 8 7
♣ A J 7 2

South	West	North	East
1 NT	Pass	3 NT	Pass
Pass	Pass		

Opening lead: ♠ 9 (Dummy plays low)

1. How many high card points does partner have?
2. Which spade do you play, and what is your plan?

NO STAYMAN? (Solution)

North
♠ Q 10 7
♡ J 10 7 2
◇ K Q J 3
♣ Q 10

West
♠ 9 4
♡ 8 4 3
◇ 9 6 5
♣ 9 6 5 4 3

East
♠ A J 6 2
♡ A 6 5
◇ 8 7
♣ A J 7 2

South
♠ K 8 5 3
♡ K Q 9
◇ A 10 4 2
♣ K 8

1. Zero! You can see 25 high card points between your hand and the dummy.
2. The ♠ A. Why didn't declarer cover partner's lead with the ♠ 10—the normal play? There can only be one answer. Declarer is trying to bait you into ducking this trick. Don't do it!

    Make the stronger play of the ♠ A followed by the ♣ A and a club. There is only one chance to defeat this contract and that is to play declarer for ♣ Kx and attack the suit before the ♡ A is dislodged.

    Even the kibitzers will be impressed.

KEY LESSON POINTERS

1. WHEN DECLARER MAKES AN IMPOSSIBLE PLAY FROM DUMMY, DO NOT PLAY HASTILY. IF DECLARER IS COMPETENT, YOU ARE BEING SET UP.
2. WHEN DECLARER HAS ALL OF THE MISSING POINTS, IT IS EASY ENOUGH TO COUNT THE OPPONENT'S TRICKS. THE IDEA IS TO KNOW WHAT TO DO AFTER YOU HAVE COUNTED THEM.
3. PARTNERS ARE PERMITTED TO TRY SHORT SUIT LEADS VS. NOTRUMP IF THEIR OWN SUIT LOOKS HOPELESS. IN THIS PARTICULAR CASE, TRUSTY OLD FOURTH BEST WOULD HAVE WORKED AGAIN.

(32) TWO CUE BIDS (1) (2)

East-West vulnerable
Dealer West

North
♠ Q 4
♡ K Q J
◇ A 10 5 3
♣ 5 4 3 2

West (you)
♠ 10 7 5
♡ 10
◇ Q J 9 8
♣ A K Q J 10

West	North	East	South
1 ♣	Pass	Pass	1 ♠
Pass	2 ♣	Pass	2 ◇
Pass	3 ♣	Pass	3 ♡
Pass	5 ◇	Pass	Pass
Pass			

Opening lead: ♣ Q

You continue with a second club and declarer ruffs. Declarer plunks down the ◇ K, partner following, and continues with a low diamond. You split your honors; declarer ducks in dummy, and partner discards a low heart.

1. What do you play now?
> You continue with a third club which declarer ruffs.
> Declarer now plays three top spades discarding a club from dummy, partner playing the ♠ 6, ♠ 8, and ♠ J. Declarer continues with the ♠ 9.

2. What do you do now?
> You discard your heart, as do partner and dummy. Declarer now plays another spade.

3. What is declarer's distribution?
4. What do you play now?

TWO CUE BIDS (Solution)

North
♠ Q 4
♡ K Q J
◇ A 10 5 3
♣ 5 4 3 2

West
♠ 10 7 5
♡ 10
◇ Q J 9 8
♣ A K Q J 10

East
♠ J 8 6
♡ 9 6 5 4 3 2
◇ 2
♣ 8 7 6

South
♠ A K 9 3 2
♡ A 8 7
◇ K 7 6 4
♣ 9

3. Declarer is known to be 5-3-4-1.
4. You have already made the key discard of your lone heart. All you have to do is discard once again. Declarer will have to lead a heart and you can ruff.

   Declarer has misplayed the hand by not cashing one heart earlier, but you still had to take advantage of his error.

   Had you discarded a club on the fourth spade instead of your heart, declarer might have awakened and cashed the ♡ A before playing his last spade.

   Worst of all is to ruff either the fourth or fifth spade. Dummy overruffs, your last trump is drawn and you get no more tricks.

KEY LESSON POINTERS

1. IF YOUR OPPONENTS NEVER MAKE A MISTAKE AGAINST YOU, YOU CANNOT BE A WINNING PLAYER. BESIDES, YOU ARE PROBABLY SITTING TOO CLOSE TO THE TABLE.
2. ONE WAY TO AVOID A TRUMP COUP IS TO DISCARD FROM YOUR SHORTEST SIDE SUIT ON WINNERS IT IS NOT SAFE TO RUFF. DECLARER WILL NO LONGER BE ABLE TO CASH WINNERS IN THAT SUIT.

(33) SEEING IT ALL (1)

Neither side vulnerable
Dealer South

North
♠ Q J 6 2
♡ K Q 5 4
◇ Q 3
♣ 7 5 4

East (you)
♠ A 10 9
♡ 9 8
◇ A 8 7 6 4
♣ 8 3 2

South	West	North	East
1 NT	Pass	2 ♣	Pass
2 ♡	Pass	4 ♡	Pass
Pass	Pass		

Opening lead: ♣ Q

Declarer wins the ♣ A and plays a heart to the king, a heart to the jack and, finally, the ♡ 10 as you discard a diamond. The ◇ 10 is led to the queen, partner playing the deuce.
  1. How do you proceed?
     You win the ◇ A and exit a club to declarer's king, partner playing the ♣ 9.
     Declarer plays off the ◇ K J, partner following, and discards a club from dummy. Declarer exits with the ♠ 5, partner plays the ♠ 4 and dummy the ♠ Q.
  2. Do you win this trick? If so, what do you return?

SEEING IT ALL (Solution)

North
♠ Q J 6 2
♡ K Q 5 4
◊ Q 3
♣ 7 5 4

West
♠ K 8 4
♡ 7 6 3
◊ 9 5 2
♣ Q J 10 9

East
♠ A 10 9
♡ 9 8
◊ A 8 7 6 4
♣ 8 3 2

South
♠ 7 5 3
♡ A J 10 2
◊ K J 10
♣ A K 6

2. Win the trick and play a club. Declarer must ruff in dummy and lead a spade. You now collect three spades and a diamond.

   Declarer has shown up with 16 points outside of spades, so partner is marked with the ♠ K. Declarer's red suit distribution is known, so you must work out the black suit distribution.

   If declarer has two spades and four clubs there is no defense because a club return sets up declarer's long club, a spade return sets up dummy's ♠ J and a diamond allows declarer to ruff in his hand and lead up to dummy's ♠ J. So, assume three spades and three clubs.

KEY LESSON POINTERS

1. WHEN DECLARER CAN HAVE ONE OF TWO POSSIBLE DISTRIBUTIONS, PLAY FOR THE ONE THAT ALLOWS YOU TO DEFEAT THE CONTRACT.

2. THE FACT THAT DUMMY HAS A VOID SUIT ALONG WITH A TRUMP OR TWO, DOES NOT MEAN YOU SHOULD NEVER ATTACK SUCH A SUIT. AT TIMES IT IS THE BEST PLAY. HERE IT LOCKS DECLARER IN DUMMY AND FORCES HIM TO LEAD A SUIT FROM DUMMY (SPADES), THAT HE WOULD RATHER BE LEADING FROM HIS HAND.

(34) TWO FOR ONE

Neither side vulnerable
Dealer East

North
♠ 4 3 2
♡ J 10
♢ 9 7 6 4 3
♣ A 10 7

West (you)
♠ 8 6 5
♡ 9 4 2
♢ Q 8 5 2
♣ Q 3 2

East	South	West	North
1 ♡	Dbl.	Pass	2 ♢
2 ♡	2 ♠	Pass	3 ♠
Pass	4 ♠	Pass	Pass
Pass			

Opening lead: ♡ 2

Partner wins the ♡ Q and ♡ K and shifts to the ♢ J. Declarer wins the ♢ A and draws trumps in three rounds, partner discarding a heart on the third trump. Declarer continues with the ♢ K and ♢ 10, partner discarding another heart on the ♢ K.

1. What is declarer's distribution?
2. How do you plan your defense?

TWO FOR ONE (Solution)

North
♠ 4 3 2
♡ J 10
◇ 9 7 6 4 3
♣ A 10 7

West
♠ 8 6 5
♡ 9 4 2
◇ Q 8 5 2
♣ Q 3 2

East
♠ 9 7
♡ A K Q 7 5 3
◇ J
♣ K 9 8 5

South
♠ A K Q J 10
♡ 8 6
◇ A K 10
♣ J 6 4

1. 5-2-3-3. If declarer had a third heart, he would have ruffed it in dummy before drawing trumps.
2. Duck the ◇10. If you take the trick, declarer has an easy road to ten tricks: five spades, four diamonds and a club. If you duck, declarer will be unable to use the diamonds and, depending upon the club spots, may have to lose two tricks in that suit. In fact, he does.

KEY LESSON POINTERS

1. WHEN DECLARER REMOVES ALL OF DUMMY'S TRUMPS, ASSUME DE-CLARER HAS NO LOSERS TO RUFF IN ANY SHORT SIDE SUIT THE DUMMY MAY HAVE.
2. ENTRY CONSIDERATIONS MAY MAKE IT WORTHWHILE TO SACRIFICE A TRICK TO PREVENT DECLARER FROM ESTABLISHING A BLOCKED SUIT.

(35) WRONG LEAD (1)

East-West vulnerable
Dealer West

North
♠ Q 4 3
♡ J 5 4
◇ 3 2
♣ A K Q J 9

West (you)
♠ A J 6 5 2
♡ —
◇ K 10 7 4
♣ 10 6 3 2

West	North	East	South
Pass	1 ♣	2 ♡ *	2 NT**
Pass	3 NT	Pass	Pass
Pass			

*Weak
**10-12

Opening lead: ♠ 5

Dummy plays low, partner plays the ♠ 8 and declarer wins the ♠ 10.

1. At trick two declarer leads the ♠ 7. Which spade do you play? Why?

   You rise with the ♠ A in order to block the suit if declarer started with four spades.

   Partner discards the ♡ 8 on the ♠ A.

2. Thrilled that your partner wants you to return a heart, what do you play at trick three?

WRONG LEAD (Solution)

North
♠ Q 4 3
♡ J 5 4
◇ 3 2
♣ A K Q J 9

West
♠ A J 6 5 2
♡ —
◇ K 10 7 4
♣ 10 6 3 2

East
♠ 8
♡ A Q 10 8 7 3
◇ Q J 6 5
♣ 7 5

South
♠ K 10 9 7
♡ K 9 6 2
◇ A 9 8
♣ 8 4

2. The ◇ 4. Declarer is known to have five club tricks along with three spade tricks. However, spades are blocked so you must try to remove declarer's side entry to the spades—before he can unblock the suit.

Your diamond shift wins whenever you can run four diamond tricks (impossible in view of partner's discard), or whenever declarer has the ◇ A and partner the ♡ A and ◇ Q J.

KEY LESSON POINTERS

1. WHEN DECLARER HAS A BLOCKED SUIT, KNOCK OUT THE ENTRY TO THE HAND THAT HAS THE GREATER LENGTH IN THE BLOCKED SUIT BEFORE THE SUIT CAN BE UNBLOCKED.
2. COUNTING DECLARER'S TRICKS IS THE KEY TO WINNING DEFENSE.
3. UNLESS YOU ARE PLAYING TOURNAMENT BRIDGE, DO NOT WORRY ABOUT ALLOWING DECLARER TO MAKE OVERTRICKS. THINK IN TERMS OF DEFEATING THE CONTRACT.

(36) CRUMMY DUMMY (1)

Both sides vulnerable
Dealer South

North
♠ Q 5
♡ J 10 9
◇ Q 8 6 5 3
♣ Q J 8

West (you)
♠ J 9 8 4 3
♡ A 6
◇ 4 2
♣ K 6 5 3

South	West	North	East
1 NT	Pass	2 NT	Pass
3 NT	Pass	Pass	Pass

Opening lead: ♠ 4

Dummy plays low and partner's ♠ 2 drives out the ♠ K. Declarer continues with the ace, jack and a low diamond, partner winning the third round as you discard a club.

Partner returns the ♠ 7 which runs to the ♠ Q, declarer playing the ♠ 10. Declarer leads the ♣ Q from dummy; partner plays the ♣ 4 and declarer the ♣ 2.

1. Do you win this trick? If so, what do you return?
    You win the trick and return the ♡ A. Partner plays the ♡ 2 and declarer the ♡ 3.
2. What do you play next?

CRUMMY DUMMY (Solution)

North
♠ Q 5
♡ J 10 9
◇ Q 8 6 5 3
♣ Q J 8

West
♠ J 9 8 4 3
♡ A 6
◇ 4 2
♣ K 6 5 3

East
♠ 7 6 2
♡ K Q 8 2
◇ K 10 9
♣ 9 7 4

South
♠ A K 10
♡ 7 5 4 3
◇ A J 7
♣ A 10 2

2. The ♡ 6. Notice that partner did not insult you by "wasting" the ♡ 8 when you led the ace. He "knew" you would be able to work out the heart continuation. How did he know?

Because he knew you could count tricks. He knew you could count three spades, four diamonds and two clubs—so what chance other than hearts? Plus 200 is better than plus 100.

Of course, players that use upside down attitude signals would have had no trouble. Under the lead of the ♡ A, the ♡ 2 screams for a continuation. (Commercial.)

KEY LESSON POINTERS

1. WHEN THIRD HAND HAS THREE SMALL CARDS (8xx OR WORSE), IT IS MORE HELPFUL TO PLAY LOW AND GIVE COUNT THAN IT IS TO PLAY "THIRD HAND HIGH."
2. WHEN IT IS OBVIOUS THAT DECLARER HAS NINE TRICKS AVAILABLE IN THREE SUITS, ATTACK THE FOURTH SUIT AND THEN LOOK TO SEE WHAT YOU HAVE IN THAT SUIT. THIS IS A RECORDING.
3. AT TIMES PARTNER CANNOT AFFORD TO SIGNAL ENCOURAGEMENT WITHOUT WASTING A TRICK. GOOD DEFENDERS ALLOW FOR THIS POSSIBILITY—PARTICULARLY WHEN PARTNER IS APT TO HAVE FOUR CARDS IN THE SUIT.

(37) RAPID FIRE (1) (2)

East-West vulnerable
Dealer South

North
♠ A K Q 8 6 4
♡ 10 2
◇ Q 6
♣ J 10 9

East (you)
♠ J 9 7 3
♡ Q 8 3
◇ K 9 4 3
♣ Q 5

South	West	North	East
2 ♡ *	Pass	Pass	Pass

*Weak 7-10

Opening lead: ♣ K

1. Which club do you play at trick one?
   You play the ♣ Q.
   At trick two partner cashes the ♣ A and continues with the ♣ 2, which you ruff low, declarer playing the ♣ 4, ♣ 6, and ♣ 7.
2. What do you play now?
   The ◇ K which holds. You continue with a low diamond to partner's ace and partner produces the ♣ 3. Declarer discards a spade from dummy.
3. What do you play on the ♣ 3?

RAPID FIRE (Solution)

North
♠ A K Q 8 6 4
♡ 10 2
◊ Q 6
♣ J 10 9

West	East
♠ 10 2	♠ J 9 7 3
♡ J 5	♡ Q 8 3
◊ A 8 7 5	◊ K 9 4 3
♣ A K 8 3 2	♣ Q 5

South
♠ 5
♡ A K 9 7 6 4
◊ J 10 2
♣ 7 6 4

3. Uppercut declarer with the ♡ Q. You need one more trick to defeat the contract and it must come from the trump suit.

   If declarer has the ♡ A K J, there is no defense, but if partner has the ♡ J, your play of the ♡ Q will promote that card to the setting trick.

KEY LESSON POINTERS

1. SIGNALLING HIGH LOW WITH A DOUBLETON QUEEN IS A RARITY. THE PLAY OF THE QUEEN UNDER THE KING NORMALLY SHOWS THE JACK. HOWEVER WHEN THE JACK IS IN THE DUMMY, THIRD HAND IS ALLOWED TO HIGH-LOW WITH Qx.
2. RUFFING UNNECESSARILY HIGH MAY PROMOTE A TRUMP TRICK FOR PARTNER. THIS PLAY IS CALLED AN "UPPERCUT" AND IS MOST SUCCESSFUL WHEN PARTNER HAS AN EQUIVALENT OR EVEN A LOWER TRUMP HONOR. BE ON THE LOOKOUT FOR "UPPERCUTS."

(38) THREE I CAN SEE

Neither side vulnerable
Dealer East

North
♠ A Q 9 4 3
♡ A 10 2
◇ K Q
♣ Q 6 2

East (you)
♠ 5
♡ J 9 8 7 6 4
◇ A 5 3
♣ A K 8

East	South	West	North
1 ♡	1 ♠	Pass	4 ♠
Pass	Pass	Pass	

Opening lead: ♡ 3

Declarer wins the ♡ K, draws two rounds of trumps, and continues by cashing the ♡ Q and the ♡ A, partner discarding the ◇ J and ◇ 2.

Declarer exits with a diamond from dummy which you win. You return a diamond, all following.

1. At this point declarer leads a low club from dummy. What is declarer's distribution, and which club do you play?

THREE I CAN SEE (Solution)

North
♠ A Q 9 4 3
♡ A 10 2
◇ K Q
♣ Q 6 2

<table>
<tr><td>

West
♠ 8 2
♡ 3
◇ J 10 9 8 4 2
♣ J 9 7 4
</td><td>

East
♠ 5
♡ J 9 8 7 6 4
◇ A 5 3
♣ A K 8
</td></tr>
</table>

South
♠ K J 10 7 6
♡ K Q 5
◇ 7 6
♣ 10 5 3

1. 5-3-2-3. Partner's discards will be discussed below. Play the ♣ 8. You need three club tricks to defeat the contract and your only real hope is that partner has the ♣ J. Of course, it is possible that declarer has J9x and will mistakenly play the ♣ 9. After all, you are marked with both club honors to justify an opening bid.

    In any case, you cannot lose your ♣ A K, as declarer is marked with three clubs.

KEY LESSON POINTERS

1. HONOR DISCARDS SUCH AS THE ◇ J ARE NOT COUNT DISCARDS. THEY SIMPLY INDICATE A COMPLETE SEQUENCE, USUALLY WITH NO HIGHER HONOR.
2. AFTER AN HONOR DISCARD (OR AN ATTITUDE DISCARD), THE SECOND DISCARD IN THAT SUIT INDICATES PRESENT COUNT—HOW MANY CARDS YOU HAVE IN THE SUIT BEFORE YOU MAKE THE SECOND DISCARD.

EXAMPLES:

A. HOLDING J 10 9 8 4 2
DISCARD THE JACK AND THEN THE DEUCE. THE JACK SHOWS THE SEQUENCE AND THE DEUCE INDICATES AN ODD NUMBER OF CARDS REMAINING AT TIME OF THE SECOND DISCARD.

B. HOLDING J 10 9 8 7
DISCARD THE JACK AND THEN THE 10. WHEN THE SECOND DIS-
CARD IS A HIGH SPOT CARD IT INDICATES AN EVEN NUMBER OF
CARDS REMAINING.

C. HOLDING 8 4 3 2
DISCARD THE DEUCE (ATTITUDE), AND THEN THE THREE, PRESENT
COUNT.

D. HOLDING 8 6 4 3 2
DISCARD THE DEUCE (ATTITUDE), AND THEN THE SIX OR EIGHT,
PRESENT COUNT.

(39) SOME SUIT!

Both sides vulnerable
Dealer East

North
♠ J 10 9 4
♡ 3 2
◇ A 9 3
♣ 9 6 5 4

East (you)
♠ A Q 3 2
♡ —
◇ K 10 8
♣ A K J 8 7 3

East	South	West	North
1 ♣	4 ♡	Pass	Pass
Dbl.	Pass	Pass	Pass

Opening lead: ♣ 2

Declarer ruffs and plays the ♡ A K, partner playing the ♡ 10 and ♡ 9.

1. What is partner's heart holding?

   At trick four declarer plays the ♠ K, partner playing the ♠ 5.

2. What is declarer's distribution?
3. Do you take this trick? If so, what do you return?

SOME SUIT! (Solution)

North
♠ J 10 9 4
♡ 3 2
◇ A 9 3
♣ 9 6 5 4

West	East
♠ 8 6 5	♠ A Q 3 2
♡ Q 10 9	♡ —
◇ J 7 6 5	◇ K 10 8
♣ Q 10 2	♣ A K J 8 7 3

South
♠ K 7
♡ A K J 8 7 6 5 4
◇ Q 4 2
♣ —

1. Q 10 9. With J 10 9 partner plays J-9.
2. 2-8-3-0. Partner's ♠ 5, a count card, indicates three small.
3. Yes. The ◇ K in order to kill the spade suit. For this play to succeed your partner needs the ◇ J to go along with the ♡ Q.
   If you lead any other diamond, declarer will win the ◇ Q and continue spades. Now you win zero diamond tricks. Similarly, if you play a club, declarer will ruff, knock out your ♠ Q and again you will not get a single diamond trick—both of declarer's diamonds going off on the spades.

KEY LESSON POINTERS

1. HOLDING AN HONOR SEQUENCE OF THREE OR MORE CARDS IN THE TRUMP SUIT, PLAY HIGHEST-LOWEST WHEN FOLLOWING SUIT. FOR EXAMPLE, FROM Q J 10 9, PLAY THE QUEEN AND THEN THE NINE.
2. WHEN LEADING OR FOLLOWING SUIT WITH THREE OR FIVE TRUMPS, PLAY HIGH-LOW IF YOU WISH TO GIVE COUNT. WITH TWO OR FOUR TRUMPS PLAY UP THE LINE.
3. IN CERTAIN INSTANCES A HIGH-LOW IN THE TRUMP SUIT INDICATES THE DESIRE TO RUFF. WHEN RUFFING IS UNLIKELY, THE COUNT INTERPRETATION PREVAILS.
4. SOMETIMES A KING MUST BE SACRIFICED TO KILL A DUMMY ENTRY. A NOBLER DEATH CANNOT BE ENVISIONED.
5. IF EAST-WEST NEEDED TWO QUICK DIAMOND TRICKS (HERE THEY NEED BUT ONE), EAST MUST SHIFT TO THE ◇ 10, CATERING TO Jxx IN THE SOUTH HAND.

(40) CONGESTION (1)

Both sides vulnerable
Dealer South

North
♠ J 9 3 2
♡ J 8 2
◇ K 10 7 6
♣ Q 10

West (you)
♠ K 7 6 5
♡ A K Q 10
◇ 8
♣ K 9 8 2

South	West	North	East
1 ◇	Dbl.	2 ◇	Pass
2 ♠	Pass	3 ♠	Pass
4 ♠	Pass	Pass	Pass

Opening lead: ♡ Q

You continue with the ♡ K and ♡ A, declarer ruffing the third heart with the ♠ 4.

1. At trick four declarer leads the ♠ Q. What do you do?
   You duck the trick, partner playing the ♠ 8. Declarer continues with the ♠ 10.
2. Do you win this trick? If so, what do you return?

CONGESTION (Solution)

North
♠ J 9 3 2
♡ J 8 2
◇ K 10 7 6
♣ Q 10

West	East
♠ K 7 6 5	♠ 8
♡ A K Q 10	♡ 7 6 5 3
◇ 8	◇ 9 5
♣ K 9 8 2	♣ J 7 6 5 4 3

South
♠ A Q 10 4
♡ 9 4
◇ A Q J 4 3 2
♣ A

2. Win the trick and return a diamond. No matter what declarer has, he will not be able to unblock his ♠ A and return to dummy to remove your last trump.
   Your diamond play will have removed a valuable dummy entry prematurely.

KEY LESSON POINTERS

1. BE ON THE LOOKOUT FOR BLOCKED SUITS. HERE THE TRUMP SUIT IS BLOCKED. BY REMOVING THE LONE ENTRY TO THE DUMMY PREMATURELY, YOU INSURE A SECOND TRUMP TRICK.
2. WHEN HOLDING FOUR TRUMPS TO A HIGH HONOR, IT IS USUALLY RIGHT TO LEAD FROM YOUR LONGEST, RATHER THAN YOUR SHORTEST, SIDE SUIT. HOWEVER, IF THE BIDDING HAS INDICATED THAT DECLARER HAS EXTREME TRUMP LENGTH, GO FOR THE RUFFS INSTEAD.

(41) SPOT WATCHER

Both sides vulnerable
Dealer North

North
♠ A J 4 3
♡ 9 4
◊ J 6 4
♣ A K J 10

East (you)
♠ K 9 5 2
♡ 6 5
◊ A K 7 2
♣ 7 6 5 2

North	East	South	West
1 ♣	Pass	1 ♡	Pass
1 ♠	Pass	4 ♡	Pass
Pass	Pass		

Opening lead: ◊ 3

You win the ◊ K and declarer plays the ◊ 5. Now what?

SPOT WATCHER (Solution)

North
♠ A J 4 3
♡ 9 4
♢ J 6 4
♣ A K J 10

West
♠ 10 8 6
♡ Q 7 3
♢ Q 10 8 3
♣ 9 8

East
♠ K 9 5 2
♡ 6 5
♢ A K 7 2
♣ 7 6 5 2

South
♠ Q 7
♡ A K J 10 8 2
♢ 9 5
♣ Q 4 3

Underlead the ♢ A by returning the ♢ 2. If partner has the expected ♢ Q and shifts to a spade you will defeat the contract with two diamonds, a spade and a trump.

How do you know partner has the ♢ Q? Two reasons: (1) the lead of a low spot card generally promises a high honor; (2) if declarer has ♢ Q 5 doubleton, partner would have started with ♢ 10 9 8 3 and would have led the ♢ 10.

Yes, if partner has led low from three small and has the ♠ Q, your shift is disastrous. On the other hand, if partner has ♢ Qxx and ♡ Jxx, a low diamond return is the only defense. Partner wins and returns a diamond. You now play a fourth diamond and promote partner's ♡ J for the setting trick.

All in all, you stand to gain more often than lose by returning a low diamond at trick two.

KEY LESSON POINTERS

1. THE LEAD OF A LOW SPOT CARD IN AN UNBID SUIT GENERALLY PROMISES A HIGH HONOR. TRUE, MANY LEAD LOW FROM THREE OR FOUR SMALL BUT GOOD PLAYERS TRY TO AVOID LEADING LOW FROM WORTHLESS SUITS.
2. THE SPOT CARDS PLAYED TO A TRICK ARE OFTEN QUITE REVEALING. PAY ATTENTION.
3. WHEN PARTNER MAKES A SEEMINGLY DARING UNDERLEAD, HE WANTS YOU TO LEAD A SUIT HE DARE NOT, OR CAN NOT, LEAD HIMSELF. EITHER THAT, OR HE HAS PULLED A WRONG CARD.

(42) LOUSY BIDDING

East-West vulnerable
Dealer South

North
♠ A K 5
♡ Q 9 8 7
◇ Q J 10 9 8
♣ 8

East (you)
♠ J 10
♡ 5 4 3 2
◇ A 7
♣ A K Q 3 2

South	West	North	East
1 ♣	Pass	1 ◇	Pass
1 NT*	Pass	2 ♡	Pass
3 ◇	Pass	3 NT**	Pass
Pass	Pass		

*Does not deny a four card major if opener has 4-3-3-3
or 3-4-3-3 distribution.
**Should bid 3 ♠.

Opening lead: ♡ J

Declarer wins the ♡ K and leads a low diamond to dummy, partner playing the deuce. Assume you win the trick. Now what?

LOUSY BIDDING (Solution)

North
♠ A K 5
♡ Q 9 8 7
♢ Q J 10 9 8
♣ 8

West
♠ 7 4 3 2
♡ J 10
♢ 4 3 2
♣ 9 6 5 4

East
♠ J 10
♡ 5 4 3 2
♢ A 7
♣ A K Q 3 2

South
♠ Q 9 8 6
♡ A K 6
♢ K 6 5
♣ J 10 7

The problem is declarer's club length. If declarer has only three clubs the hand is easily beaten by cashing three top clubs and leading a fourth round which partner will win. The club suit is blocked, but so what? You defeat the contract one trick.

However, if declarer has four clubs, it is far better to attack with a *low* club. If declarer has either 109xx or J9xx a low club return should net five club tricks. If you bang down your clubs from the top you will score only three club tricks. How can you tell?

Back to the bidding and the lead. There are eight spades missing between declarer's hand and partner's hand. If partner had five spades he probably would have led the unbid major. Assume spades are 4-4. If that assumption is correct, then declarer has only three clubs. Some players rebid a notrump with 4-3-3-3 distribution, but most players rebid one spade with 4-4 in the blacks.

You don't have much else to go on, so play your clubs from the top.

KEY LESSON POINTERS

1. KNOW YOUR OPPONENT'S BIDDING HABITS. WILL THEY OR WON'T THEY SKIP OVER A FOUR CARD MAJOR TO REBID 1 NT WITH A 4-3-3-3 HAND PATTERN? ASK, OR RESIGN YOURSELF TO DOING SOME FANCY GUESSING.

2. VS. NOTRUMP WHEN THERE ARE EIGHT CARDS MISSING BETWEEN DECLARER'S AND PARTNER'S HANDS IN THE UNBID SUIT (A MAJOR) ASSUME 4-4 DISTRIBUTION IF PARTNER LEADS ANOTHER SUIT.

(43) GOING FOR BROKE

Neither side vulnerable
Dealer West

North
♠ —
♡ A K Q
◇ A Q J 5 4 3
♣ A 8 6 2

West (you)
♠ A K J 10 9 8
♡ J 7
◇ K 9
♣ K 9 4

West	North	East	South
1 ♠	Dbl.	Pass	2 ♣
2 ♠	3 ♠	Pass	3 NT
Pass	4 ♣	Pass	5 ♣
Pass	6 ♣	Pass	Pass
Pass			

Opening lead: ♠ K

Dummy ruffs, partner plays the ♠ 3 and declarer the ♠ 4. Declarer continues with the ♣ A and a club to the queen, partner following with the ♣ 5 and ♣ 10.
Plan your defense.

GOING FOR BROKE (Solution)

North
♠ —
♡ A K Q
◇ A Q J 5 4 3
♣ A 8 6 2

West	East
West	**East**
♠ A K J 10 9 8	♠ 3 2
♡ J 7	♡ 10 8 5 4 3 2
◇ K 9	◇ 8 7 2
♣ K 9 4	♣ 10 5

South
♠ Q 7 6 5 4
♡ 9 6
◇ 10 6
♣ Q J 7 3

Win the ♣ K and continue with the ♠ A, forcing dummy to ruff. With declarer stranded in dummy, declarer's only hope is to ruff his third heart winner low, draw your last trump, and take the diamond finesse.

However, you frustrate this line by overtrumping the third heart.

If you duck the ♣ K or return anything other than a high spade, declarer makes the hand easily.

If you duck, declarer plays on in diamonds and you make no more than the ♣ K. If you return a heart, declarer draws your last trump and runs the diamonds via a finesse.

KEY LESSON POINTERS

1. WHEN YOU ARE DEFENDING AGAINST A DUMMY THAT IS EXTREMELY STRONG AND A DECLARING HAND THAT IS EXTREMELY WEAK, TRY TO PREVENT DECLARER FROM GETTING TO THE WEAK HAND TO TAKE WINNING FINESSES.
2. WHEN DUMMY IS VOID IN A SUIT, PICTURE THE SITUATION IF YOU FORCE DUMMY TO RUFF. YOU MAY BE ABLE TO VISUALIZE THAT IT WILL BE DIFFICULT FOR DECLARER TO GET OFF DUMMY SAFELY.

(44) TIME

North-South vulnerable
Dealer West

North
♠ A 4
♡ J 3
◇ K 7 6 5 3
♣ K J 3 2

East (you)
♠ Q J 7 5
♡ A 10 9 8
◇ A J 10 8
♣ 4

West	North	East	South
Pass	Pass	1 ◇	1 NT*
Pass	3 NT	Pass	Pass
Pass			

*15-18

Opening lead: ♠ 10

Dummy wins the opening lead, as you signal with the ♠ 7. At trick two a low diamond is led from dummy.
1. How many high card points does partner have?
2. Which diamond do you play, and what is your plan?

TIME (Solution)

North
♠ A 4
♡ J 3
◇ K 7 6 5 3
♣ K J 3 2

<table>
<tr><td>

West
♠ 10 9 8 3 2
♡ 7 5 4 2
◇ —
♣ 9 8 6 5

</td><td>

East
♠ Q J 7 5
♡ A 10 9 8
◇ A J 10 8
♣ 4

</td></tr>
</table>

South
♠ K 6
♡ K Q 6
◇ Q 9 4 2
♣ A Q 10 7

1. Zero. Even if South plays 15-17 notrump overcalls, partner cannot have a point. You can see 24 high card points between your hand and dummy. If declarer has only 15, partner has one. But you can see all four jacks, so partner can't even have that.

2. The ◇ A and return a high spade. Count declarer's tricks, knowing he has every missing honor card. If you duck the diamond, playing the ten or jack, declarer will win and revert to hearts scoring four clubs, two hearts, two spades and one diamond. However, if you rise with the ◇ A and return a spade honor, declarer will wind up with an extra diamond trick, but no heart tricks. He will not have time to develop the hearts.

KEY LESSON POINTERS

1. WHEN YOU KNOW DECLARER'S POINT COUNT, IT IS SIMPLE TO WORK OUT PARTNER'S. JUST ADD YOUR POINTS TO DUMMY'S POINTS TO DECLARER'S POINTS AND SUBTRACT FROM 40. WHAT'S LEFT BELONGS TO PARTNER.

2. WHEN DECLARER HAS ONLY ONE STOPPER REMAINING IN YOUR LONG SUIT AND TWO CARDS TO KNOCK OUT, BE WARY OF LETTING HIM STEAL A TRICK IN ONE SUIT BEFORE HE ATTACKS ANOTHER. IN THIS CASE YOU CAN COUNT HIS TRICKS AND PREVENT HIM FROM STEALING A DIAMOND BEFORE HE REVERTS TO HEARTS.

3. IT GOES WITHOUT SAYING THAT YOU HAVE TO BE AWAKE WHEN YOU PLAY THIS GAME.

(45) COLLISION

East-West vulnerable
Dealer North

North
♠ A 4
♡ A K 4
◇ Q J
♣ K Q J 10 9 8

West (you)
♠ J 10 9 8 7
♡ J 10 9
◇ A 10 8 2
♣ A

North	East	South	West
1 ♣	Pass	1 NT	2 ♠
3 NT	Pass	Pass	Pass

Opening lead: ♠ J

Dummy wins, partner playing the ♠ 3 and declarer the ♠ Q.
At trick two the ♣ K goes to your ♣ A, partner playing the ♣ 2.
What do you play at trick three?

COLLISION (Solution)

North
♠ A 4
♡ A K 4
◇ Q J
♣ K Q J 10 9 8

<table>
<tr><td>

West
♠ J 10 9 8 7
♡ J 10 9
◇ A 10 8 2
♣ A

</td><td>

East
♠ 6 5 3
♡ 8 7 6 5
◇ K 4 3
♣ 7 3 2

</td></tr>
</table>

South
♠ K Q 2
♡ Q 3 2
◇ 9 7 6 5
♣ 6 5 4

The ◇ A. Declarer has nine tricks staring you in the face; five clubs, two spades and at least two hearts. In order to defeat this contract you must cash four diamonds. Ergo, partner must have the ◇ K.

Even so, you must be careful. You must cash the ◇ A and then lead a diamond to partner's king in case declarer has 9xxx. If you lead a low diamond originally, declarer's presumed 9xxx will stand up as a fourth round stopper.

Yes, if partner has specifically ◇ K 9 doubleton, you must shift to a low diamond. No letters, please.

KEY LESSON POINTERS

1. YOU CAN'T EVEN BEGIN TO CALL YOURSELF A BRIDGE PLAYER UNTIL YOU TRAIN YOURSELF TO COUNT THEIR TRICKS.
2. WHEN DECLARER CAN READILY MAKE HIS CONTRACT BY CASHING WINNERS IN THREE SUITS, ATTACK THE FOURTH SUIT.
3. WHEN ATTACKING THE FOURTH SUIT, KNOW HOW MANY TRICKS YOU NEED IN THE SUIT AND WHICH HONOR OR HONOR CARDS YOU MUST FIND IN PARTNER'S HAND AND PLAY ACCORDINGLY.
4. WHEN DUMMY HAS A POWERFUL SIDE SUIT MISSING THE ACE, PLUS A CERTAIN ENTRY (OR TWO) TO THE SUIT, THE PARTNER OF THE PLAYER WITH THE ACE (IN THIS CASE, EAST), SHOULD NOT GIVE COUNT WHEN THE SUIT IS LED, HE SHOULD GIVE SUIT PREFERENCE.

(46) INVITATION ACCEPTED

Both sides vulnerable
Dealer East

North
♠ A 7 3
♡ K J 8 6 4 2
♢ 6
♣ 9 5 3

West (you)
♠ Q J 10 9
♡ 9 7 5
♢ A 7
♣ A J 4 2

East	South	West	North
Pass	1 NT	Pass	2 ◊ *
Pass	2 ♡	Pass	3 ♡
Pass	4 ♡	Pass	Pass
Pass			

*Transfer bid.

Opening lead: ♠ Q

Declarer wins in dummy, partner contributing the ♠ 2.
At trick two declarer leads a diamond to the king, partner playing the ◊ 10. You win the trick—nice play—now what?

INVITATION ACCEPTED (Solution)

North
♠ A 7 3
♡ K J 8 6 4 2
♢ 6
♣ 9 5 3

West
♠ Q J 10 9
♡ 9 7 5
♢ A 7
♣ A J 4 2

East
♠ 8 5 2
♡ 10
♢ 10 9 8 5 4 2
♣ K 7 6

South
♠ K 6 4
♡ A Q 3
♢ K Q J 3
♣ Q 10 8

Lead a low club. Partner has denied the ♠ K and has shown you via the ♢ 10 that declarer has the ♢ K Q J. (More about that below).

If your inferences are correct, your best chance is to play partner for one card, the ♣ K, and switch before your club winners go bye-bye on the diamonds.

KEY LESSON POINTERS

1. IN MOST CASES, WHEN AN HONOR CARD IS LED AT TRICK ONE, THIRD HAND GIVES AN ATTITUDE, NOT A COUNT, SIGNAL.

2. WHEN IT COMES TO SPLITTING HONORS BY SECOND HAND, HERE IS A SIMPLE IDEA THAT WORKS WELL IN PRACTICE: SPLIT WITH THE SAME HONOR YOU WOULD HAVE LED, HAD YOU BEEN ON LEAD. YOUR HONOR HOLDING WILL BE FAR CLEARER TO PARTNER THAN IF YOU SPLIT WITH THE LOWER OR LOWEST HONOR, THE TRADITIONAL WAY OF SPLITTING.

   HOW IS PARTNER TO KNOW, FOR EXAMPLE, IF YOU SPLIT WITH THE NINE WHETHER YOU HOLD QJ109, J109x, OR K Q J 10 9? HE ISN'T.

3. THIS METHOD CAN ALSO BE USED WHEN DISCARDING FROM AN HONOR SEQUENCE. DISCARD THE ONE YOU WOULD HAVE LED HAD YOU BEEN ON LEAD. YOU CAN GO EVEN FURTHER WITH THIS RULE. SAY YOU HAVE Q 10 9 8 AND YOU EITHER MUST DISCARD FROM THE SUIT OR ARE SECOND HAND. PLAY THE ONE YOU WOULD HAVE LED. IF YOU LEAD THE TEN FROM THIS COMBINATION, SPLIT WITH THE TEN OR DISCARD THE TEN. IF YOU LEAD THE NINE, SPLIT WITH THE NINE OR DISCARD THE NINE.

(47) GAMBLING 3 NT OPENING BID

Neither side vulnerable
Dealer West

North
♠ A K Q 2
♡ 8 4 3 2
♢ A K 9 2
♣ 2

            East (you)
            ♠ J 9 7 5
            ♡ J 7 5
            ♢ 10 5 4
            ♣ 6 4 3

West	North	East	South
3 NT*	Dbl.	4 ♣**	4 ◊
Pass	5 ◊	Pass	Pass
Pass			

    *Solid minor plus one outside stopper.
    **Rescue mission

    Opening lead: ♣ Q (From A K Q)

You play low, count, and partner continues with the ♣ A showing an odd number of clubs originally. Declarer ruffs the club continuation low in dummy, cashes the ◊ A, all following, and leads a diamond to his queen, partner pitching a club.

Declarer continues by cashing three top spades, partner discarding a club on the third and leads a low heart from dummy.

1. What is declarer's distribution?
2. Which heart do you play?

GAMBLING 3 NT OPENING BID (Solution)

North
♠ A K Q 2
♡ 8 4 3 2
◇ A K 9 2
♣ 2

West
♠ 8 6
♡ K 10 9
◇ 3
♣ A K Q J 9 8 7

East
♠ J 9 7 5
♡ J 7 5
◇ 10 5 4
♣ 6 4 3

South
♠ 10 4 3
♡ A Q 6
◇ Q J 8 7 6
♣ 10 5

1. 3-3-5-2. Partner has given you the count in clubs and has shown out in both diamonds and spades. If you don't know declarer's distribution by now, chances are you never will.
2. The ♡ J. In order to defeat this contract you need two heart tricks. The only critical combination is ♡ AQx in declarer's hand and ♡ K 10 9 in partner's.

   If you don't play the ♡ J, declarer can play low and force partner to win the trick. With partner on lead, either a heart or a club return will be fatal.

KEY LESSON POINTER

1. NO MATTER HOW FRUSTRATING, YOU MUST TRY TO KEEP COUNTING DECLARER'S DISTRIBUTION. EVENTUALLY YOU WILL SUCCEED. LET'S HOPE YOU ARE NOT TOO OLD TO ENJOY THE FRUITS OF YOUR LABOR.
2. IN THE END GAME, SECOND HAND MUST FREQUENTLY PLAY HIGH TO GET PARTNER OFF AN END PLAY.
3. WHEN DECLARER FINALLY GETS AROUND TO PLAYING WHAT APPEARS TO BE THE CRITICAL SUIT, YOU MUST KNOW HOW MANY TRICKS YOU NEED IN THAT SUIT AND WHAT MINIMUM HONOR HOLDING PARTNER NEEDS IN THAT SUIT TO DEFEAT THE CONTRACT. THEN PLAY ACCORDINGLY.

(48) WEAK JUMP SHIFT IN COMPETITION

Neither side vulnerable
Dealer East

North
♠ J 9 5
♡ J 10 7 5 2
◇ A K 10 6
♣ 3

East (you)
♠ K 10 2
♡ 8
◇ 9 5
♣ A K Q J 9 8 7

East	South	West	North
1 ♣	1 ♠	3 ◇ *	Dbl. * *
4 ♣	4 ♡	Pass	Pass
Pass			

*Not forcing
* *Penalty

Opening lead: ♣ 10

Plan your defense.

WEAK JUMP SHIFT IN COMPETITION (Solution)

North
♠ J 9 5
♡ J 10 7 5 2
◇ A K 10 6
♣ 3

West
♠ 4 3
♡ A 6
◇ Q J 8 7 4 3 2
♣ 10 6

East
♠ K 10 2
♡ 8
◇ 9 5
♣ A K Q J 9 8 7

South
♠ A Q 8 7 6
♡ K Q 9 4 3
◇ —
♣ 5 4 2

Overtake and shift to a low spade. The lead of the ♣ 10 marks declarer with at least three clubs. The strength of dummy's diamonds indicates partner has a seven card suit. If this is all true, declarer's most likely distribution is 5-5-0-3.

So how can you defeat this contract? Leading a low spade works whenever partner has ♠ Ax, or ♠ Qx and a trump trick. It also works when you scare declarer into thinking you have a singleton spade.

Once you get that idea in his head, he will rise with the ♠ A and knock out your ♡ A thinking he has avoided a spade ruff. Won't he feel foolish when he sees you give partner a spade ruff rather than vice-versa?

When you come to think of it, you have little chance of defeating this contract other than trying to con declarer. (If partner had two trump tricks, he would have doubled 4 ♡.)

KEY LESSON POINTERS

1. WHEN DEFEATING A CONTRACT BY LEGITIMATE MEANS LOOKS HOPE-LESS, CONSIDER A SWINDLE. THEY'RE SO MUCH FUN WHEN THEY WORK.
2. IN ORDER TO PERPETUATE A SUCCESSFUL SWINDLE, YOU MUST PLAY ON DECLARER'S FEARS. FOR EXAMPLE, WHEN LOOKING AT EIGHT OR NINE CARDS IN A SUIT BETWEEN THE TWO HANDS, DECLARERS ARE ALWAYS AFRAID DEFENDERS ARE SWITCHING TO SINGLETONS.
3. REMEMBER—DECLARER CANNOT SEE YOUR HAND. IT'S NOT WHAT YOU HAVE THAT MATTERS, IT'S WHAT DECLARER THINKS YOU HAVE.

(49) THOSE LONG SUITS

Both sides vulnerable
Dealer North

North
♠ 8 6 3
♡ K
◇ A K Q 10 9 8
♣ A Q 3

East (you)
♠ A 4
♡ Q 9 2
◇ 7 6 5 3
♣ 10 8 6 4

North	East	South	West
1 ◇	Pass	1 ♡	1 ♠
3 ◇	Pass	3 NT	Pass
Pass	Pass		

Opening lead: ♠ Q

Plan your defense.

THOSE LONG SUITS (Solution)

North
♠ 8 6 3
♡ K
◇ A K Q 10 9 8
♣ A Q 3

<table>
<tr><td>

West
♠ Q J 10 9 2
♡ A J 8 3
◇ J
♣ J 9 7

</td><td>

East
♠ A 4
♡ Q 9 2
◇ 7 6 5 3
♣ 10 8 6 4

</td></tr>
</table>

South
♠ K 7 5
♡ 10 7 6 5 4
◇ 4 2
♣ K 5 2

Win the opening lead and shift to the ♡ 9! You can see nine tricks in plain view outside of the heart suit; six diamonds, one spade and at least two clubs. What chance other than cashing four hearts do you have? Right. None.

In order to cash four heart tricks your partner needs to hold ♡ AJ8x or AJ8xx. Even with this magic holding you must begin by unblocking the ♡ 9.

How will partner work this out? Faith. He can count tricks as well. He will know that if you don't have the ♡ Q, declarer has nine tricks even without the ♣ K; six diamonds, one spade, one heart and one club. Faith.

KEY LESSON POINTERS

1. WHEN IT IS CLEAR THAT DECLARER CAN MAKE HIS CONTRACT WITH ENOUGH WINNING TRICKS IN THREE SUITS, ATTACK THE FOURTH SUIT—EVEN IF YOU NEED A MINOR MIRACLE IN THE SUIT TO SUCCEED.
2. SOMETIMES MINOR MIRACLES REQUIRE AN UNBLOCK FROM AN ORIGINAL THREE CARD HOLDING HEADED BY ONE HONOR AND A HIGH MIDDLE SPOT CARD.
3. MANY PLAYERS HAVE ADOPTED THE LEAD OF THE Q FROM K Q 10 COMBINATIONS VS. NOTRUMP. THE LEAD ASKS PARTNER TO UNBLOCK THE JACK IF HE HAS IT. AS VALUABLE A CONVENTION AS THIS IS, IT SHOULD NOT BE USED WHEN EITHER DUMMY OR DECLARER IS KNOWN TO HAVE A LONG STRONG SUIT. IN THOSE CASES LEADING THE KING WORKS BEST. TO UNDERSTAND WHY, CONSIDER EAST'S DILEMMA AT TRICK ONE IF HE COULD NOT BE SURE WHETHER WEST HAS LED FROM A K/Q 10 COMBINATION OR TOP OF A SEQUENCE.

(50) WHERE? (1)

Neither side vulnerable
Dealer West

North
♠ A J 3 2
♡ K Q 9 8 7
◇ Q 2
♣ Q 10

West (you)
♠ K Q 6
♡ A 6
◇ J 10 9 3
♣ A 9 8 7

West	North	East	South
1 ◇	Dbl.	Pass	2 ♠
Pass	3 ♠	Pass	4 ♠
Pass	Pass	Pass	

Opening lead: ♡ A

You continue with the ♡ 6, declarer winning in his hand with the ♡ J, partner playing the ♡ 4 and ♡ 5 .
1. At trick three declarer leads a low spade. Which spade do you play?
   You split your honors and dummy's ace wins, partner playing the ♠ 10. At trick four a low spade is led from dummy to declarer's ♠ 9, partner discarding the ♣ 6.
2. How do you continue?

WHERE? (Solution)

North
♠ A J 3 2
♡ K Q 9 8 7
◇ Q 2
♣ Q 10

West	East
♠ K Q 6	♠ 10
♡ A 6	♡ 10 5 4
◇ J 10 9 3	◇ 8 7 6
♣ A 9 8 7	♣ K 6 5 4 3 2

South
♠ 9 8 7 5 4
♡ J 3 2
◇ A K 5 4
♣ J

2. Lead a low club to partner's king and get your heart ruff. Partner's ♣ 6 is a giant club. There are four lower clubs missing and partner is sure to have some of those lower clubs. Once you know that partner has the ♣ K you can see four defensive tricks—if declarer has a third heart.

   Do not make the mistake of leading the ♣ A first. If declarer has a singleton club you will have removed partner's entry!

KEY LESSON POINTERS

1. WHEN TRYING TO DETERMINE WHETHER PARTNER'S SPOT CARD DISCARD IS AN ENCOURAGING SIGNAL OR NOT, LOOK BENEATH THE CARD. IF THERE ARE A NUMBER OF LOWER CARDS NOT VISIBLE BETWEEN YOUR HAND AND DUMMY, ASSUME AN ENCOURAGING SIGNAL IS BEING MADE.
2. DO NOT BE AFRAID TO UNDERLEAD AN ACE TO GET PARTNER IN FOR A RUFF. IF DECLARER HAS A SINGLETON IT MAY BE THE ONLY WAY.
3. PARTNER'S PLAYS IN HEARTS (HIS LOWEST) ALSO INDICATE CLUB STRENGTH. WHENEVER PARTNER HAS WORTHLESS CARDS IN A SUIT YOU ARE KNOWN TO BE SHORT, HIS CARDING SHOULD BE DIRECTED TOWARD SUIT PREFERENCE.

Section IV
PLAY

THE DENT IN THE ARMOR (Solution)
(problem on back cover)

North
♠ Q 10 3 2
♡ 4 2
◊ K J 9 8
♣ K J 10

West
♠ A 4
♡ K Q 10 8
◊ A 6 5
♣ 6 5 4 3

East
♠ 9 8 6 5
♡ 9 7 6 3
◊ Q 10 3 2
♣ 2

South
♠ K J 7
♡ A J 5
◊ 7 4
♣ A Q 9 8 7

The ◊ 5. You can see 23 high card points between your hand and the dummy. Declarer has at least 15 so your partner has either a queen or two jacks at most.

As partner has denied the ♡ J by playing a low heart at trick one, you can forget about partner having two jacks and concentrate on his having one queen.

If it is the ♣ Q it won't do you any good. Declarer won't bother with clubs. He will simply knock out both mssing aces. As you have them both you will never be able to get your partner in for a heart play. Furthermore, if you continue hearts from your side, the most you can hope for is two heart tricks along with your two aces.

No, the best bet is to hope partner has the ◊ Q and shift to a low card in that suit. If declarer does not play the ◊ K at trick two, partner will be on lead to shift to a heart dooming the contract.

If declarer rises with the ◊ K, you still have one last gasp. You have to hope partner started with ◊ Q 10xx. Now when declarer drives out the ♠ A, you can play ace and a diamond collecting three diamonds, a heart and a spade. What a truly great defender you are.

(26) VULNERABLE SACRIFICE

North-South vulnerable
Dealer West

North
♠ K Q J 6 3
♡ Q J 9 6 4
♢ Q
♣ 7 2

South
♠ A 10 8 5
♡ K 10 8 3
♢ K 8 7 6
♣ 5

West	North	East	South
1 ♣	*2 ♣	2 ♢	4 ♡
5 ♣	Pass	Pass	5 ♡
Dbl.	Pass	Pass	Pass

*Majors

Opening lead: ♢ 10

East wins the ♢ A and shifts to the ♠ 9. Plan the play.

VULNERABLE SACRIFICE (Solution)

North

♠ K Q J 6 3
♡ Q J 9 6 4
◊ Q
♣ 7 2

West

♠ 7 4 2
♡ A
◊ 10 2
♣ A Q J 10 9 6 3

East

♠ 9
♡ 7 5 2
◊ A J 9 5 4 3
♣ K 8 4

South

♠ A 10 8 5
♡ K 10 8 3
◊ K 8 7 6
♣ 5

East has apparently shifted to a singleton. If you win and play a trump, there is a good chance that West will win, give East a spade ruff, win the club return and give East a second spade ruff. Down two.

There is a way to hold this to a one trick set. Win the spade in your hand, play the ◊ K, discarding a club from the table and play a third diamond. If West shows out, discard the last club from the table.

Since you have deprived East of a club entry to the West hand, East will be able to get but one spade ruff. Your vulnerable sacrifice will have worked, because the opponents can make five clubs.

KEY LESSON POINTERS

1. TRANSFERRING LOSERS FROM ONE DEFENSIVE HAND TO ANOTHER IS ONE WAY OF AVOIDING A RUFF.
2. HERE THE IDEA IS TO LOSE AN EXTRA DIAMOND TRICK TO EAST, RATHER THAN A LATER CLUB TRICK TO WEST. WEST CAN USE HIS ENTRY TO GIVE EAST A SPADE RUFF. EAST CAN DO NOTHING TO HURT YOU WITH HIS.

(27) VERY SCARY

North-South vulnerable
Dealer East

North
♠ 6 4
♡ A 7 6 5
◊ K J 10
♣ K J 8 3

South
♠ Q 7 3
♡ K Q 10
◊ Q 9 8 2
♣ A 10 2

East	South	West	North
2 ♠ *	Pass	Pass	Dbl.
Pass	3 NT	Pass	Pass
Pass			

*weak

Opening lead: ♠ K

East overtakes and continues with the ♠ J, West following.
You win the ♠ Q and cash the ♡ K Q, East following with the
♡ 3 and ♡ J.
What is your plan from here?

VERY SCARY (Solution)

North
♠ 6 4
♡ A 7 6 5
◇ K J 10
♣ K J 8 3

West
♠ K 2
♡ 9 8 4 2
◇ 5 4 3
♣ Q 9 7 4

East
♠ A J 10 9 8 5
♡ J 3
◇ A 7 6
♣ 6 5

South
♠ Q 7 3
♡ K Q 10
◇ Q 9 8 2
♣ A 10 2

East is playing like a man with the ◇ A, so you must forget about developing diamonds and concentrate on scoring four club tricks instead.

West should have the ♣ Q. East, presumed to hold the ◇ A, has shown nine high card points and might well have opened 1 ♠ rather than 2 ♠ had he the ♣ Q as well.

Therefore, you should cash the ♣ A and run the ♣ 10 if not covered. If the ♣ Q is covered, return to your hand with the ♡ 10 and lead your remaining club towards dummy's ♣ J 8. Assuming West follows low, finesse the ♣ 8. As East is marked with long spades, he figures to be shorter in clubs than West. Play the odds.

KEY LESSON POINTERS

1. GIVE THIRD HAND CREDIT FOR HAVING SOMETHING IN MIND WHEN HE OVERTAKES PARTNER'S KING, ESTABLISHING YOUR QUEEN.
2. MOST PLAYERS WILL NOT OPEN A WEAK TWO BID HOLDING 11 or 12 HIGH CARD POINTS PLUS A GOOD SUIT. THEY WILL OPEN WITH A ONE BID.

(28) TOUGH GUESS?

East-West vulnerable
Dealer North

North
♠ 9 7 6
♡ A K Q 10 2
◇ K J 5
♣ A Q

South
♠ K 5 3
♡ 9 4
◇ 6 4
♣ K J 9 7 6 2

North	East	South	West
1 ♡	Pass	1 NT	Pass
3 NT	Pass	Pass	Pass

Opening lead: ◇ 3

Which diamond do you play from dummy? Why?

TOUGH GUESS? (Solution)

North
♠ 9 7 6
♡ A K Q 10 2
◇ K J 5
♣ A Q

West
♠ A 10 4 2
♡ J 7
◇ A 10 8 3 2
♣ 5 3

East
♠ Q J 8
♡ 8 6 5 3
◇ Q 9 7
♣ 10 8 4

South
♠ K 5 3
♡ 9 4
◇ 6 4
♣ K J 9 7 6 2

The ◇ K. It's easy to lose sight of the ball on this one. The problem is really not diamonds. It's spades!

What you want to do is decrease the chance of East winning the lead and shifting to a spade through your king. Obviously, if East has the ◇ A you cannot keep him off lead, but if he has the ◇ Q, you can. For that reason you must go up with the ◇ K. If the ◇ K loses to the ace you are going to have to sweat out the spade position.

Why put yourself under the gun when you don't have to?

KEY LESSON POINTERS

1. WHEN YOU FEAR A SHIFT TO ANOTHER SUIT, AND AN OPPONENT IS LEADING THROUGH A K J COMBINATION, YOU CAN DECREASE THE LIKELIHOOD OF THE SHIFT BY FLYING WITH THE KING.

2. THE SAME PRINCIPLE IS INVOLVED WHEN A K J COMBINATION IS BEING LED THROUGH AND THE PARTNER OF THE PLAYER LEADING THE SUIT HAS THE SETTING TRICK(S) BEHIND THE K J. GO UP WITH THE KING. IF THE PLAYER WITH THE SETTING TRICK(S) HAS THE ACE, THE HAND CAN'T BE MADE, BUT IF HIS PARTNER HAS THE ACE YOU MAY STILL BE ABLE TO MAKE THE CONTRACT.

(29) NOTRUMP PREFERRED

East-West vulnerable
Dealer South

North
♠ Q J 9 6 3
♡ J 5 2
◇ A Q 7
♣ J 2

South
♠ 7 2
♡ A Q 9 8 7
◇ K 2
♣ K Q 10 3

South	West	North	East
1 ♡	Pass	1 ♠	Pass
2 ♣	Pass	3 ♡	Pass
4 ♡	Pass	Pass	Pass

Opening lead: ♠ K

East plays the ♠ 4 (attitude) at trick one. Which spade do you play? Why?

NOTRUMP PREFERRED (Solution)

North
♠ Q J 9 6 3
♡ J 5 2
◇ A Q 7
♣ J 2

West	East
♠ A K 5	♠ 10 8 4
♡ K 6	♡ 10 4 3
◇ 9 8 6 3	◇ J 10 5 4
♣ 9 8 5 4	♣ A 7 6

South
♠ 7 2
♡ A Q 9 8 7
◇ K 2
♣ K Q 10 3

The ♠ 2. You wish to discard your other spade on a diamond. In order to do this, you must encourage West to shift.

If you play the ♠ 2, West will be sure that his partner has made a discouraging signal and may shift to a diamond, presenting you with the contract.

KEY LESSON POINTERS

1. AS DECLARER, SIGNAL THE OPENING LEADER AS IF HE WERE YOUR PARTNER! PLAY HIGH IF YOU WANT THE OPENING LEADER TO CONTINUE THE SUIT HE HAS LED, PLAY LOW IF YOU DON'T.
2. IN GENERAL, CONCEALING LOW SPOT CARDS IS GOOD STRATEGY. IT CREATES CONFUSION. THIS HAND IS AN EXCEPTION.

(30) KEEPING TRACK (1) (2)

North-South vulnerable
Dealer West

North

♠ Q 7 4 3
♡ A Q 4
◇ 2
♣ A K J 4 3

South

♠ A K 5
♡ K J 8 7 6
◇ K Q 6
♣ 5 2

West	North	East	South
Pass	1 ♣	2 ◇ *	2 ♡
Pass	4 ◇ * *	Pass	4 NT* * *
Pass	5 ♠ * * * *	Pass	6 NT
Pass	Pass	Pass	

*Weak
* *Splinter
* * *Key Card Blackwood
* * * *Two key cards with the ♡ Q.

Opening lead: ◇ 3

After much thought East produces the ◇ 7 which you top with the ◇ K.
1. Which suit do you attack first?
   You race off five rounds of hearts, East discarding three diamonds and a club, dummy two clubs, and West, the ◇ 5.
2. How do you proceed?
   You cash a club, all following, and then play three rounds of spades ending in *your* hand. On the third spade, West discards a club.
3. How do you continue?

KEEPING TRACK (Solution)

North
♠ Q 7 4 3
♡ A Q 4
◇ 2
♣ A K J 4 3

West	East
♠ 10 2	♠ J 9 8 6
♡ 10 9 3 2	♡ 5
◇ 5 4 3	◇ A J 10 9 8 7
♣ Q 10 9 6	♣ 8 7

South
♠ A K 5
♡ K J 8 7 6
◇ K Q 6
♣ 5 2

3. Take the club finesse. East is marked with six diamonds from the bidding and the lead, and has turned up with four spades and a heart, leaving him a grand total of two clubs.

   As East has followed to one club and discarded another, you don't have to be an Einstein to work out that East is now void in clubs. What you have to do is COUNT.

KEY LESSON POINTERS

1. USE THE BIDDING AND THE LEAD TO HELP WITH THE COUNT AND HONOR PLACEMENT.
2. YOU ARE WITHIN YOUR RIGHTS TO TRY TO WORK OUT WHY EAST IS HESITATING AT TRICK ONE. IN THIS CASE IT IS OBVIOUS THAT HE IS DEBATING ABOUT PLAYING THE ◇ A.
3. IF DISCARDING ON YOUR OWN LONG SUIT WILL NOT PRESENT PROBLEMS, RUN THE LONG SUIT BEFORE FIDDLING WITH SUITS THAT ARE MISSING QUEENS (CLUBS), OR JACKS (SPADES). THE OPPONENTS' DISCARDS MAY BE QUITE REVEALING.

(31) FAVORABLE LEAD

Neither side vulnerable
Dealer South

North
♠ Q 10 4 2
♡ K 10 7
◇ Q 10
♣ K J 9 3

South
♠ K J 9 3
♡ Q 8 5 4
◇ K 7
♣ A Q 8

South	West	North	East
1 NT	Pass	3 NT	Pass
Pass	Pass		

Opening lead: ♡ 9

Which heart do you play from dummy? Why?

FAVORABLE LEAD (Solution)

North
♠ Q 10 4 2
♡ K 10 7
◇ Q 10
♣ K J 9 3

<table>
<tr><td>

West
♠ A 8
♡ 9 6 2
◇ 9 6 5 4 2
♣ 5 4 2

</td><td>

East
♠ 7 6 5
♡ A J 3
◇ A J 8 3
♣ 10 7 6

</td></tr>
</table>

South
♠ K J 9 3
♡ Q 8 5 4
◇ K 7
♣ A Q 8

The ♡ 7. It is very likely that East has AJx or AJxx of hearts and you want to encourage him to duck this trick so you can knock out the ♠ A before anyone finds a diamond shift.

Although East should smell a rat when you don't play the ♡ 10 from dummy, many East players would routinely play low on the ♡ 7. Once you have avoided a trick two diamond shift, the hand is a piece of cake.

KEY LESSON POINTERS

1. IF YOU WISH TO DISCOURAGE THIRD HAND FROM WINNING THE OPENING LEAD, MAKE A PLAY FROM DUMMY THAT WILL ENCOURAGE HIM NOT TO WIN THE TRICK. IN OTHER WORDS, PLAY LOW.
2. LOOK AT THE ENTIRE HAND BEFORE YOU PLAY FROM DUMMY TO THE FIRST TRICK. HERE, AS FAR AS HEARTS ARE CONCERNED, IT IS CLEARLY BETTER TO PLAY THE ♡ 10. HOWEVER, AS FAR AS THE WHOLE HAND IS CONCERNED, IT IS BETTER TO PLAY LOW IN ORDER TO ENCOURAGE A DEFENSIVE ERROR.
3. WHEN DUMMY COMES DOWN AND YOU SUSPECT THAT YOU ARE NOT IN THE RIGHT CONTRACT, (HERE YOU MISSED A 4-4 SPADE FIT), NEVER, BUT NEVER, SAY ANYTHING. GOOD OPPONENTS WILL PICK UP ON IT. TREAT EVERY DUMMY PARTNER PUTS DOWN WITH LOVE AND AFFECTION, YOU CAN MURDER HIM AFTER THE GAME IS OVER.

(32) DELICATE BIDDING

East-West vulnerable
Dealer South

North
♠ K Q 10
♡ Q 4
◇ 9 8 3 2
♣ K 10 5 3

South
♠ A J 5
♡ A K 7 6 3
◇ Q
♣ A 8 4 2

South	West	North	East
1 ♡	Pass	1 NT	Pass
2 ♣	Pass	2 ♠*	Pass
3 ♠	Pass	4 ♡	Pass
5 ♣	Pass	Pass	Pass

*Strong raise to 3 ♣

Opening lead: ◇ K

West continues with the ◇ A which you ruff, East playing up the line.

You play the ♣ A and a low club to dummy, allowing West to hold the ♣ J, East discarding a spade. West continues with a low diamond to East's ◇ J, which you ruff with your last trump. How do you continue?

DELICATE BIDDING (Solution)

North
♠ K Q 10
♡ Q 4
◇ 9 8 3 2
♣ K 10 5 3

West
♠ 6
♡ J 9 2
◇ A K 10 5 4
♣ Q J 9 6

East
♠ 9 8 7 4 3 2
♡ 10 8 5
◇ J 7 6
♣ 7

South
♠ A J 5
♡ A K 7 6 3
◇ Q
♣ A 8 4 2

In order to make this contract you must find West with exactly three hearts and at least one spade.

What you are going to have to do is discard dummy's losing diamond on the third heart, cash one high spade, and continue with two winning hearts. If West trumps, dummy overtrumps and dummy is high. If West refuses to trump, dummy takes the last two tricks with the ♣ K 10 over West's ♣ Q 9.

KEY LESSON POINTERS

1. WHEN AN OPPONENT HAS A FINESSABLE TRUMP HONOR, (THE GOOD NEWS), AND YOU HAVE NO TRUMP WITH WHICH TO TAKE THE FINESSE, (THE BAD NEWS), CONSIDER THE POSSIBILITY OF A TRUMP COUP.
2. IN ORDER TO PULL OFF ONE OF THESE TRUMP COUPS, YOU MUST HAVE THE SAME TRUMP LENGTH AS YOUR OPPONENT AND USUALLY YOU MUST BE LEADING WINNING CARDS THROUGH HIM. IF HE TRUMPS, OVERTRUMP; IF HE REFUSES TO TRUMP, CONTINUE PLAYING WINNING CARDS. EVENTUALLY YOU WILL TAKE THE LAST TRICKS IN THE TRUMP SUIT WITHOUT ACTUALLY FINESSING. A MIRACLE.

(33) LESSON HAND (1)

Both sides vulnerable
Dealer South

North
♠ Q J 6 2
♡ K Q 5 4
♢ Q 3
♣ 7 5 4

South
♠ 7 5 3
♡ A J 10 2
♢ K J 10
♣ A K 6

South	West	North	East
1 NT	Pass	2 ♣	Pass
2 ♡	Pass	4 ♡	Pass
Pass	Pass		

Opening lead: ♣ Q (East plays the ♣ 2.)

1. After winning the opening lead, what is your plan? (Trumps
   are 3-2)
   Draw *two* rounds of trumps and lead a diamond to the
   queen. East wins the ♢ A and continues with the ♣ 8.
2. How do you continue?

LESSON HAND (Solution)

North
♠ Q J 6 2
♡ K Q 5 4
◇ Q 3
♣ 7 5 4

<table>
<tr><td>

West
♠ K 8 4
♡ 7 6 3
◇ 9 5 2
♣ Q J 10 9

</td><td>

East
♠ A 10 9
♡ 9 8
◇ A 8 7 6 4
♣ 8 3 2

</td></tr>
</table>

South
♠ 7 5 3
♡ A J 10 2
◇ K J 10
♣ A K 6

2. Play two top diamonds, discarding a club from dummy, and lead a spade.

    You cannot afford to play a third trump. If you do, you will go down when spades are 3-3 and the honors are divided!

    Say you play a third trump and lead a spade. East wins and plays a club forcing you to ruff with dummy's last trump. Now you must play a second round of spades from the table and you lose three spade tricks.

    However, if you lead a spade first, you can take the club force in dummy, return to your hand with a trump and lead the second round of spades, from the right hand—yours. This line limits the opponents to two spades and one diamond.

KEY LESSON POINTERS

1. WHEN IT IS IMPORTANT TO USE THE TRUMP SUIT FOR LATER COM-MUNICATIONS, DEFER DRAWING TRUMPS, OR AT LEAST SOME OF THE TRUMPS.
2. WHEN HOLDING QJxx FACING xxx, PLAN TO LEAD UP TO THE QJxx TWICE.
3. WHEN DRAWING TRUMPS PRESERVE ENTRY FLEXIBILITY. FOR EXAM-PLE, WHEN YOU DRAW TWO ROUND OF TRUMPS, PLAY THE KING AND THE JACK, RETAINING A LATER TRUMP ENTRY TO EITHER HAND. IT WOULD BE FATAL TO PLAY TWO HIGH TRUMPS FROM YOUR HAND LEAVING THE BLANK K Q IN DUMMY.

(34) EVERYTHING COUNTS (1)

Neither side vulnerable
Dealer East

North
♠ Q 6
♡ 7 4 3
◇ A 10 7
♣ 9 6 5 4 3

South
♠ 8 3
♡ A K Q J 10
◇ J 8 2
♣ A K 10

East	South	West	North
1 ♠	Dbl.	Pass	2 ♣
2 ♠	3 ♡	Pass	4 ♡
Pass	Pass	Pass	

Opening lead: ♠ 2

East wins the first two spades, West following. At trick three East shifts to the ♣ J to your ♣ A. You draw three rounds of trumps, East discarding a spade on the third trump.

1. How do you continue?
    You play the ♣ K followed by the ♣ 10. Both cards win, East discarding two more spades.
2. What is East's distribution?
3. How do you continue from here?

EVERYTHING COUNTS (Solution)

North
♠ Q 6
♡ 7 4 3
◇ A 10 7
♣ 9 6 5 4 3

West
♠ 9 4 2
♡ 9 8 6
◇ Q 4 3
♣ Q 8 7 2

East
♠ A K J 10 7 5
♡ 5 2
◇ K 9 6 5
♣ J

South
♠ 8 3
♡ A K Q J 10
◇ J 8 2
♣ A K 10

2. 6-2-4-1. East's bidding has indicated a six card spade suit, and his hearts and clubs have been accounted for.

3. You are reduced to playing diamonds for one loser, keeping in mind that you have squeeze possibilities against West in the minors.

There are two ways to go about this hand. You can play West for Q9x or K9x of diamonds and lead low to the seven driving out an honor. That will be the end of the hand. However, if the seven loses to the nine, you are dead.

A second way is to lead a low diamond to the ten, playing East, the player with the diamond length, for the ◇ 9. Assume East wins the ◇ 10 as in the actual layout. What can he do? If he returns a diamond, play low from your hand and capture West's ◇ Q. If he does not return a diamond, West will be squeezed on the spade return which you will ruff.

As East has more diamonds than West, you should assume East has the ◇ 9 and lead a low diamond to the ten planning on squeezing West if a diamond is not returned.

KEY LESSON POINTERS

1. MOST HANDS COUNT OUT—BUT ONLY IF YOU PAY ATTENTION TO THE BIDDING AND THE FALL OF THE CARDS.
2. WHEN LOOKING FOR ANY PARTICULAR SPOT CARD, HERE THE ◇ 9, ASSUME THE PLAYER WHO WAS LONGER IN THE SUIT ORIGINALLY STARTED WITH THE CARD.
3. WHEN LOOKING FOR ANY PARTICULAR HONOR CARD, ASSUME THE PLAYER WHO WAS LONGER IN THE SUIT ORIGINALLY HAS THE CARD— UNLESS HIS PARTNER NEEDS THE MISSING HONOR TO JUSTIFY THE BIDDING.

(35) OOF! (1)

Both sides vulnerable
Dealer North

North
♠ J 7 6
♡ Q 4 3
◊ A K Q J 10
♣ 3 2

South
♠ K 8 4 2
♡ K 10 8 5
◊ 8 7
♣ A J 6

North	East	South	West
1 ◊	2 ♠ *	2 NT	Pass
3 NT	Pass	Pass	Pass

*Weak

Opening lead: ♡ 7

You play low from dummy, East plays the ♡ 2 and you win the ♡ 8.

1. What do you play to trick two?

   A low heart. If West ducks, you will win the ♡ Q and lead up to your ♠ K for a ninth trick.

   Alas, West rises with the ♡ A, East discarding the ♠ 5, and shifts to the ♣ 4, East producing the ♣ K.

2. What are the distributions around the table?
3. What is your plan?

OOF! (Solution)

North
♠ J 7 6
♡ Q 4 3
◇ A K Q J 10
♣ 3 2

West
♠ —
♡ A J 9 7 6
◇ 5 4 3 2
♣ Q 10 7 4

East
♠ A Q 10 9 5 3
♡ 2
◇ 9 6
♣ K 9 8 5

South
♠ K 8 4 2
♡ K 10 8 5
◇ 8 7
♣ A J 6

2. Assuming that the lead of the ♣ 4 shows a four card suit, West's distribution should be 0-5-4-4, and East's 6-1-2-4.
3. Assuming that West has the ♣ Q from East's play of the ♣ K, you are still safe even though the heart suit is blocked.

Win the ♣ A and play five rounds of diamonds, discarding three spades. This reduces all hands to five cards. Dummy will have three spades, a heart and a club, you will have one spade, two hearts and two clubs, and regardless of what West holds, you must take two more tricks.

If West holds two hearts and three clubs, or three hearts and two clubs, overtake the ♡ Q and exit with a heart. West will be forced to lead a club.

KEY LESSON POINTERS

1. USE THE BIDDING, THE LEADS, AND THE FALL OF THE CARDS TO HELP YOU COUNT THE HAND.
2. PICTURE WHAT YOUR HAND, DUMMY, AND THE OPPONENTS' HANDS WILL LOOK LIKE AFTER YOU RUN OFF A LONG SUIT. IF NECESSARY, PHYSICALLY REMOVE THE CARDS THAT YOU ARE PLANNING TO DISCARD FROM YOUR HAND TO SEE WHAT YOU WILL HAVE LEFT.

(36) FOUR LADIES IN WAITING

Neither side vulnerable
Dealer South

North
♠ Q 10 9
♡ Q 4
◇ Q 6 5 3 2
♣ Q J 8

South
♠ 8 5 4 3
♡ A K 2
◇ A J 7
♣ A 10 2

South	West	North	East
1 NT	Pass	2 NT	Pass
3 NT	Pass	Pass	Pass

Opening lead: ♡ 5

Where do you win this trick, and what is your plan?

FOUR LADIES IN WAITING (Solution)

North
♠ Q 10 9
♡ Q 4
◇ Q 6 5 3 2
♣ Q J 8

West
♠ A 7 6
♡ 10 8 6 5 3
◇ K
♣ 9 5 4 3

East
♠ K J 2
♡ J 9 7
◇ 10 9 8 4
♣ K 7 6

South
♠ 8 5 4 3
♡ A K 2
◇ A J 7
♣ A 10 2

Win the ♡ K and continue with the ◇ A and ◇ J. You must retain the ♡ Q as an entry to the diamonds, and play diamonds from the top in case one opponent has a singleton king.

After conceding a diamond (if the ◇ K is singleton, concede the third round so you don't have to discard on the fourth), win the likely heart return and run the ♣ Q. If it wins you have nine tricks, if it loses, the defenders must shift to spades and be able to take three tricks in the suit to defeat you.

KEY LESSON POINTERS

1. TRY TO RETAIN AT LEAST ONE ENTRY TO THE HAND WHICH HAS THE SUIT THAT YOU ARE ESTABLISHING.
2. WITH AJx FACING Qxxxx, THE BEST PLAY FOR *FOUR* TRICKS IS TO START WITH THE ACE. IF YOU NEED ALL FIVE, LEAD LOW TO THE JACK AND HOPE YOUR RIGHT HAND OPPONENT HAS Kx.

(37) THE FIRST FIVE (1)

East-West vulnerable
Dealer West

North
♠ J 2
♡ Q 5 2
♢ A K Q 8 6 4
♣ Q 6

South
♠ A K 9 8 7 6
♡ J 9 8
♢ 2
♣ J 10 9

West	North	East	South
Pass	1 ♢	Pass	1 ♠
Pass	2 ♢	Pass	2 ♠
Pass	Pass	Pass	

Opening lead: ♡ K

East plays the ♡ 10 at trick one and West continues with the ♡ A, East following, and, finally, a low heart, East ruffing low.

East switches to the ace and a club to West's king. West now produces a sticky fourth round of hearts.

1. How do you handle this?

As East is marked with the ♠ Q, (West has shown up with ♡ AKxxx plus the ♣ K and passed originally), there is no point in ruffing with the ♠ J. In fact, it could be disastrous. East, possibly having started with ♠ Qxx, would overtrump promoting West's presumed ♠ 10x to the setting trick.

As there is no good reason for ruffing in dummy at all, you discard a diamond. East ruffs with the ♠ Q.

2. How do you proceed from here?

THE FIRST FIVE (Solution)

North
♠ J 2
♡ Q 5 2
◇ A K Q 8 6 4
♣ Q 6

West
♠ 5 4
♡ A K 7 6 4
◇ 10 7 3
♣ K 8 7

East
♠ Q 10 3
♡ 10 3
◇ J 9 5
♣ A 5 4 3 2

South
♠ A K 9 8 7 6
♡ J 9 8
◇ 2
♣ J 10 9

2. How you continue depends to a large extent on the caliber of your opposition. If East is a player who would not dream of ruffing a high heart with the ♠ Q holding the ♠ 10 as well, overruff and run the ♠ 9, playing West for ♠ 10xx.

   If East is a very clever fellow, you simply can't tell who has the ♠ 10. As you are marked with the ♠ A K, it costs East nothing to ruff with the ♠ Q holding ♠ Q 10 doubleton. It is actually the only way to give you a problem. In real life, run the ♠ 9 after overtrumping.

KEY LESSON POINTERS

1. USE THE BIDDING TO LOCATE THE MISSING HONORS.
2. WHEN A PASSED HAND TURNS UP WITH A STRONG FIVE CARD SUIT, ASSUME THAT HAND HAS LESS THAN 12 HIGH CARD POINTS.
3. PAY OFF TO GENIUS PLAYS—THEY DON'T HAPPEN THAT OFTEN.

(38) LOOKS BAD

East-West vulnerable
Dealer East

North
♠ A K 8
♡ A K 10 8 6 4
♢ K
♣ Q 6 2

South
♠ Q J 5
♡ Q J 3 2
♢ 6 5 4
♣ 10 7 3

East	South	West	North
1 ♠	Pass	Pass	Dbl.
Pass	2 ♡	3 ♢	4 ♡
Pass	Pass	Pass	

Opening lead: ♠ 3

You win in dummy and draw trumps, East shedding a spade on the second round.

At trick four you lead a diamond to the king and East's ace. East returns the ♢ 9 which you ruff. You cross to your hand with a spade, West discarding a diamond, and ruff your last diamond, East discarding a spade.

At this point you have a high spade in dummy, a high and a low trump and three clubs. In your hand you have a spade, a high and a low trump and three clubs.

1. What is the original distribution of the opponents' hands?
2. How do you visualize the club honors?
3. How do you continue if East is the weaker player?
4. How do you continue if West is the weaker player?

LOOKS BAD (Solution)

North
♠ A K 8
♡ A K 10 8 6 4
♢ K
♣ Q 6 2

West
♠ 3
♡ 9 7
♢ Q J 10 8 7 3 2
♣ J 8 5

East
♠ 10 9 7 6 4 2
♡ 5
♢ A 9
♣ A K 9 4

South
♠ Q J 5
♡ Q J 3 2
♢ 6 5 4
♣ 10 7 3

1. East started with 6-1-2-4 and West with 1-2-7-3. You know this because you have seen one player or the other show out in three suits—and you've been counting!
2. East must have both the ace and king. West would not have passed an opening bid holding seven diamonds to the QJ10 along with a club honor, and East would not have had enough to open without the ♣ A K.
3. If East is the weaker player (doesn't count), cash the high spade and lead a low club. If East wins the trick with the king or ace, the hand can no longer be defeated.
4. If West is the weaker player (doesn't count), cash the high spade, cross to your hand with a trump and try to slip the ♣ 10 past West. If West does not cover, East will be endplayed. Of course, if East has the ♣ A K J, it doesn't matter who counts.

KEY LESSON POINTERS

1. WHEN PLAYING A HOPELESS CONTRACT LOOK FOR A LITTLE HELP.
2. IF ONE OPPONENT IS WEAKER THAN THE OTHER, MAKE THAT OPPONENT YOUR NUMBER ONE HELPER.
3. NO MATTER HOW HOPELESS A SUIT LOOKS (CLUBS), STRIP THE HAND BEFORE ATTACKING THE SUIT. WONDERFUL THINGS CAN HAPPEN; THE SUIT MAY BE BLOCKED, SOMEONE MAY DECIDE TO GIVE YOU A RUFF AND A SLUFF, ETC.

(39) DOUBLED AGAIN

East-West vulnerable
Dealer West

North
♠ 6 3
♡ J 10 9 8
♢ 9 6 5 4
♣ A 8 6

South
♠ A K J 10 9 8 7 2
♡ K 5
♢ —
♣ Q 9 7

West	North	East	South
Pass	Pass	1 ♢	4 ♠
Pass	Pass	Dbl.	Pass
Pass	Pass		

Opening lead: ♢ 2

East plays the ♢ A. What is your plan? Be specific.

DOUBLED AGAIN (Solution)

North
♠ 6 3
♡ J 10 9 8
◇ 9 6 5 4
♣ A 8 6

West	East
♠ Q 5 4	♠ —
♡ Q 6 4	♡ A 7 3 2
◇ K 10 2	◇ A Q J 8 7 3
♣ J 5 3 2	♣ K 10 4

South
♠ A K J 10 9 8 7 2
♡ K 5
◇ —
♣ Q 9 7

Assuming that West has a high diamond honor, probably the king, it is reasonable to assume that East has both the ♡ A and the ♣ K to justify his vulnerable double at the four level.

Furthermore, there is a strong likelihood that spades are 3-0, West holding the length. As you are short a dummy entry to lead up to both the ♡ K and the ♣ Q, plan to force an entry with the ♠ 6!

Ruff the lead with a middle spade and exit with a middle spade. No matter who wins, your ♠ 6 will be a second entry and you should have no further problems, losing a club, a heart, and a spade.

Do not fall into the trap of playing the ♠ A K followed by the ♡ K. East can foil this plan by winning the ♡ A and exiting with the ♣ K. Now you must lose two hearts, a club and a spade.

KEY LESSON POINTERS

1. PLAYERS WHO MAKE VULNERABLE TAKEOUT DOUBLES AT THE FOUR LEVEL, (SOME PLAY THIS AS A PENALTY DOUBLE), GENERALLY HAVE WILD DISTRIBUTION.
2. WHEN YOU HAVE A VERY POWERFUL TRUMP HOLDING, IT IS ALMOST ALWAYS RIGHT TO CONSERVE A LOW TRUMP. IT CAN BE USED TO GET TO DUMMY IF THERE IS A HIGHER TRUMP IN DUMMY; AND ONCE IN A BLUE MOON IT CAN BE USED TO THROW AN OPPONENT IN TO FORCE A FAVORABLE LEAD.

(40) NO RESPECT (1) (2)

Neither side vulnerable
Dealer South

North
♠ 10 8 6 3
♡ 9 6 5
◇ Q J 8 4
♣ Q 8

South
♠ A Q J 9
♡ 10 4
◇ A K 10 9 7 6
♣ A

South	West	North	East
1 ◇	Dbl.	2 ◇	Pass
2 ♠	Pass	3 ♠	Pass
4 ♣	Pass	4 ♠	Pass
Pass	Dbl.	Pass	Pass
Rdbl.	Pass	Pass	Pass

Opening lead: ♡ Q (Asks For Count)

West continues with the ♡ A and ♡ K, East playing high-low.
1. What card do you play at trick three?
    You ruff with the ♠ J or ♠ Q.
2. What do you play at trick four?
    The ♠ Q (or ♠ J), which holds the trick, both following.
3. What do you play at trick five?

NO RESPECT (Solution)

North
♠ 10 8 6 3
♡ 9 6 5
◇ Q J 8 4
♣ Q 8

West	East
♠ K 7 5 4	♠ 2
♡ A K Q J	♡ 8 7 3 2
◇ 5 2	◇ 3
♣ K J 10	♣ 9 7 6 5 4 3 2

South
♠ A Q J 9
♡ 10 4
◇ A K 10 9 7 6
♣ A

3. The ♠ 9. West clearly has four spades, and you cannot afford to give up control by playing the ♠ A first. If you do, West will win the third round of spades and force you to ruff a heart with dummy's last trump. You wind up losing two hearts and two spades.

   If you exit with the ♠ 9, the only return that can give you any trouble is a diamond. If West returns a diamond, unblock the ♠ A and try to return to dummy with a diamond to draw West's last trump.

   In effect, you must hope West has two diamonds.

KEY LESSON POINTERS

1. WHEN CONFRONTED WITH AN ATTACK ON YOUR TRUMP SUIT BY A DEFENDER WHO CLEARLY HAS TRUMP LENGTH, THE BEST COUNTER TO RETAIN CONTROL IS TO GIVE UP ANY CERTAIN TRUMP LOSER WHILE RETAINING TRUMPS IN BOTH HANDS. ASSUMING BOTH YOU AND DUMMY ARE VOID IN THE SUIT THAT IS BEING ATTACKED, YOU CAN TAKE THE FORCE IN THE SHORTER TRUMP HAND, USING THE LONGER TRUMP HAND TO DRAW TRUMPS.
2. DON'T EXPECT TRUMPS TO BREAK PLEASANTLY WHEN YOU ARE DOUBLED AND YOUR SIDE HAS THE MAJORITY OF THE HIGH CARD STRENGTH.
3. BE CAUTIOUS ABOUT REDOUBLING UNLESS YOU HAVE A STRONG TRUMP HOLDING AS WELL AS AN AGREEABLE PARTNER. SOMETIMES ONE'S TRAIN GETS DERAILED BEFORE IT REACHES THE STATION.

(41) MISSING HONORS (1)

Both sides vulnerable
Dealer North

North
♠ A 7 4 3
♡ 9 4
◇ J 6 4
♣ A K Q 10

South
♠ Q J
♡ A K J 10 8 2
◇ 9 5
♣ J 4 3

North	East	South	West
1 ♣	Pass	1 ♡	Pass
1 ♠	Pass	4 ♡	Pass
Pass	Pass		

Opening lead: ◇ 3

East wins the opening lead with the ◇ K and returns the ◇ 2 to the ◇ Q in the West hand. At trick three West shifts to the ♠ 6.
1. Which spade do you play from dummy? Why?
   You win the ♠ A.
2. How do you play the trump suit?

MISSING HONORS (Solution)

North
♠ A 7 4 3
♡ 9 4
♢ J 6 4
♣ A K Q 10

West
♠ 10 8 6
♡ Q 7 3
♢ Q 10 8 3
♣ 9 8 2

East
♠ K 9 5 2
♡ 6 5
♢ A K 7 2
♣ 7 6 5

South
♠ Q J
♡ A K J 10 8 2
♢ 9 5
♣ J 4 3

1. As it appears that East has underled the ♢ A, he must be doing that in order to get a spade shift. Therefore, it is pointless to play low from dummy. You have a better chance of discarding your spade on dummy's fourth club.
2. Play the ♡ A K. If the ♡ Q does not fall, play clubs and hope you can discard your losing spade before the player with the ♡ Q can ruff in. Basically, you are hoping that the player with the ♡ Q has at least three clubs. Besides if East had the ♡ Q he might have dug up a bid over 1 ♣ with 12 high card points.

KEY LESSON POINTERS

1. WHEN A DEFENSIVE PLAYER MAKES A DARING UNDERLEAD, ASSUME HE HAS A GOOD REASON AND WORK OUT WHAT IT IS.
2. CONSIDERING THE HEART SUIT IN ISOLATION, THE PROPER PLAY IS TO RUN THE ♡ 9. HOWEVER, CONSIDERING THE WHOLE HAND, THE BEST PLAY IS TO CASH THE ♡ A K AND THEN PLAY CLUBS, A COMBINATION PLAY TO INCREASE YOUR CHANCES.

(42) SPARKLING DUMMY

Both sides vulnerable
Dealer South

North
♠ A K 5
♡ Q 10 8 4
◇ A J 10 9 2
♣ 3

South
♠ Q 10 7 4
♡ A K J
◇ Q 3
♣ J 9 4 2

South	West	North	East
1 ♣	Pass	1 ◇	Pass
1 ♠	Pass	2 ♡	Pass
2 NT	Pass	3 NT	Pass
Pass	Pass		

Opening lead: ♡ 7

What is your plan?

SPARKLING DUMMY (Solution)

North
♠ A K 5
♡ Q 10 8 4
◇ A J 10 9 2
♣ 3

<table>
<tr><td>West</td><td>East</td></tr>
<tr><td>♠ J 3 2</td><td>♠ 9 8 6</td></tr>
<tr><td>♡ 7 5 3</td><td>♡ 9 6 2</td></tr>
<tr><td>◇ 7 6 4</td><td>◇ K 8 5</td></tr>
<tr><td>♣ A Q 10 7</td><td>♣ K 8 6 5</td></tr>
</table>

South
♠ Q 10 7 4
♡ A K J
◇ Q 3
♣ J 9 4 2

Play the ♠ A K Q and if the jack doesn't appear, take the diamond finesse. Given the weakness of your combined club holdings, there is too strong a chance that the opponents can reel off at least four club tricks if the diamond finesse loses. If the ♠ J drops, you will not need to risk the diamond finesse.

KEY LESSON POINTERS

1. WITH A DOUBTFUL STOPPER (OR NO STOPPER) IN ONE SUIT, GIVE YOURSELF AS MANY CHANCES AS POSSIBLE TO REALIZE YOUR CONTRACT WITHOUT LETTING THE OPPONENTS GET THE LEAD.
2. IF YOU HAD ♣ J 10 9 7 INSTEAD OF YOUR ACTUAL CLUB HOLDING, IT WOULD BE INEXCUSABLE TO PLAY SPADES BEFORE DIAMONDS. IF YOU ATTACK DIAMONDS FIRST AND THE FINESSE LOSES, THE OPPONENTS CAN ONLY TAKE THREE CLUBS AND A DIAMOND. IF YOU TEST SPADES BEFORE DIAMONDS, YOU MIGHT BE SETTING UP THE FIFTH DEFENSIVE TRICK—IF THE DIAMOND FINESSE LOSES AND SOMEONE HAS FOUR SPADES TO THE JACK.
3. YOU CAN'T PLAN THE PLAY OF THE HAND INTELLIGENTLY UNLESS YOU KNOW HOW MANY TRICKS THE OPPONENTS CAN TAKE ONCE THEY GET THE LEAD.

(43) NO KIDDING? (1)

East-West vulnerable
Dealer West

North
♠ —
♡ A K Q
◇ A Q J 6 5 4
♣ A 7 3 2

South
♠ J 8 7 6
♡ 9 5 3
◇ 10 2
♣ Q J 9 8

West	North	East	South
1 ♠	Dbl.	Pass	2 ♣
2 ♠	5 NT	Pass	6 ♣
Pass	Pass	Pass	

Opening lead: ♠ K

You ruff low in dummy, East playing the ♠ 2.
1. How do you continue?
   You lead a low club to the queen and king.
2. West continues with the ♠ A. Now what?

NO KIDDING? (Solution)

North

♠ —
♡ A K Q
◇ A Q J 6 5 4
♣ A 7 3 2

West	East
♠ A K Q 10 9 3	♠ 5 4 2
♡ J 7	♡ 10 8 6 4 2
◇ K 9 3	◇ 8 7
♣ K 6	♣ 10 5 4

South

♠ J 8 7 6
♡ 9 5 3
◇ 10 2
♣ Q J 9 8

2. You don't have much choice. Ruff with the ♣ A and lead a club to the nine. If East has either ♣ 10x or 10xx, and West the ◇ K, you make the hand. If not, tomorrow is another day.

Incidentally, leading the ◇ Q at trick two, trying to create an entry to your hand with the ◇ 10, is an inferior play. Although it works the way the cards lie, it loses whenever East has the ♣ K, or if you later misguess the club position.

KEY LESSON POINTERS

1. WHEN THERE IS A SCARCITY OF ENTRIES TO THE LONGER TRUMP HOLDING, TRY TO KEEP A FLEXIBLE POSITION IN THE TRUMP SUIT.

ON THIS HAND, FOR EXAMPLE, YOU HAVE TWO WAYS OF GOING WRONG. IF YOU PLAY ACE AND A CLUB AT TRICKS TWO AND THREE, WEST CAN WIN AND PLAY A SPADE LOCKING YOU IN DUMMY.

SIMILARLY, IF AFTER LEADING A CLUB AT TRICK TWO TO WEST'S KING, YOU RUFF HIS SPADE RETURN LOW IN DUMMY, YOU WILL BE STUCK THERE AFTER CASHING THE NOW BLANK ♣ A.

2. DESPERATE CONTRACTS CALL FOR DESPERATE MEASURES.

(44) TOUGH LEAD (1)

North-South vulnerable
Dealer West

North
♠ A 4
♡ J 3
♢ K 10 8 7 6
♣ K J 4 2

South
♠ K 6
♡ K Q 6 2
♢ Q 5 4
♣ A Q 9 7

West	North	East	South
Pass	Pass	1 ♢	1 NT
Pass	3 NT	Pass	Pass
Pass			

Opening lead: ♠ 10

1. Where do you win this trick, and what do you play at trick two?

   You win in dummy and lead a low heart to your king which holds.
2. Now what?

TOUGH LEAD (Solution)

North
♠ A 4
♡ J 3
◇ K 10 8 7 6
♣ K J42

West
♠ 10 9 8 3 2
♡ 9 8 5 4
◇ 2
♣ 6 5 3

East
♠ Q J 7 5
♡ A 10 7
◇ A J 9 3
◇ 10 8

South
♠ K 6
♡ K Q 6 2
◇ Q 5 4
♣ A Q 9 7

2. Cross to dummy with a club and lead a low diamond. If East plays the ◇ A and continues spades, you have nine tricks, one heart, two-diamonds, two spades and four clubs. If East plays low, win the ◇ Q and revert back to hearts while you still have a spade stopper. After driving out the ♡ A you have nine tricks; two hearts, one diamond, four clubs and two spades.

   The trick here is to set up three winners in the red suits before your second spade stopper is removed.

KEY LESSON POINTERS

1. THERE IS AN ADVANTAGE IN LEADING TOWARDS AN HONOR, RATHER THAN LEADING AN HONOR. CONSIDER THE HEART SUIT. YOU ARE ONLY ENTITLED TO TWO TRICKS, BUT IF YOU LEAD LOW TOWARDS YOUR HAND, EAST MUST PLAY LOW OR ELSE YOU WILL GET THREE HEART TRICKS. ONCE YOU HAVE "STOLEN" A HEART TRICK YOU CAN USE THE SAME TECHNIQUE IN DIAMONDS--LEAD TOWARDS THE QUEEN. ONCE AGAIN EAST MUST PLAY LOW OR GIVE YOU AN EXTRA DIAMOND TRICK. ONCE YOU HAVE "STOLEN" A DIAMOND YOU CAN REVERT BACK TO HEARTS AND SCORE THREE RED SUIT TRICKS BEFORE YOUR LAST STOPPER HAS BEEN REMOVED. WHAT A THIEF YOU ARE.

2. IF YOU LEAD A DIAMOND AT TRICK TWO, EAST CAN RISE WITH THE ACE AND RETURN A SPADE HONOR DEFEATING THE CONTRACT. LEADING A DIAMOND AT TRICK TWO GIVES YOU TWO DIAMONDS BUT NO HEART TRICKS BEFORE YOUR SPADE STOPPER IS REMOVED. LEADING HEARTS FIRST IS BETTER. IF EAST RISES WITH THE ♡ A, YOU GET THREE HEART TRICKS.

(45) IMPRESSIVE DUMMY

East-West vulnerable
Dealer North

North
♠ A 4
♡ A Q J
◇ K Q J 10 9 7
♣ Q J

South
♠ K J 2
♡ K 6 5
◇ 6 5 3
♣ 9 7 6 4

North	East	South	West
1 ◇	Pass	1 NT	Pass
3 NT	Pass	Pass	Pass

Opening lead: ♠ 6

1. Are there any combinations of cards that can defeat you? If so, what are they?
2. What is your plan?

IMPRESSIVE DUMMY (Solution)

North

♠ A 4
♡ A Q J
◇ K Q J 10 9 7
♣ Q J

West	East
♠ Q 9 8 6 3	♠ 10 7 5
♡ 10 9 4	♡ 8 7 3 2
◇ A	◇ 8 4 2
♣ 10 8 5 3	♣ A K 2

South

♠ K J 2
♡ K 6 5
◇ 6 5 3
♣ 9 7 6 4

1. Yes. If West has either ♣ 108xx, ♣ K108x or ♣ A108x the hand can be defeated if the opponents shift to a club after winning the ◇ A. However, in the latter two cases West must play his high honor first.

    In order to avoid a potentially disastrous club shift, conceal your spade strength. One way is to win the ♠ A underplaying the ♠ J. This might convince the opponents to continue spades rather than shift to clubs upon winning the ◇ A.

KEY LESSON POINTERS

1. WHEN YOU FEAR A SHIFT, MASK YOUR STRENGTH IN THE SUIT THAT HAS BEEN LED—EVEN IF IT MEANS SACRIFICING A TRICK (AN OVERTRICK) IN THE SUIT THAT HAS BEEN LED.
2. WINNING A TRICK IN DUMMY IS MORE DECEPTIVE THAN WINNING IN THE CLOSED HAND. IF YOU PLAY LOW FROM DUMMY, THE OPENING LEADER HAS A BETTER IDEA OF WHAT IS GOING ON WHEN HE CAN SEE PARTNER'S "THIRD HAND HIGH" PLAY.

(46) BLESSED

East-West vulnerable
Dealer South

North
♠ K J 10 9 8 7
♡ 6 4 2
♢ 4
♣ A 6 3

South
♠ A Q 6
♡ Q 9 3
♢ K Q J
♣ K 8 4 2

South	West	North	East
1 NT*	Pass	4 ♡ **	Pass
4 ♠	Pass	Pass	Pass

*15-17
**Transfer

Opening lead: ♣ Q

What is your plan?

BLESSED (Solution)

North

♠ K J 10 9 8 7
♡ 6 4 2
◇ 4
♣ A 6 3

West	**East**
♠ 5 4 3	♠ 2
♡ A J 7	♡ K 10 8 5
◇ A 7 5	◇ 10 9 8 6 3 2
♣ Q J 10 9	♣ 7 5

South

♠ A Q 6
♡ Q 9 3
◇ K Q J
♣ K 8 4 2

You have been blessed with the ♣ 4 and the ♣ 2, two clubs lower than any club East can produce at trick one.

By winning the ♣ A in dummy and underplaying the ♣ 8, you are sure to fool West into thinking that whatever card his partner plays at trick one is an encouraging signal in clubs.

In order to take advantage of this situation lead a diamond at trick two. If West has the ◇ A, he is more likely to continue clubs than he is to shift to a low heart, the only defense that can defeat the contract the way the cards lie.

From West's point of view, you might have something like:

♠ AQx ♡ K10xx ◇ KQJx ♣ xx

If so, a club continuation followed by a heart through the king is the only defense to defeat the contract.

KEY LESSON POINTERS

1. RETAINING SPOT CARDS LOWER THAN THE ONE PLAYED BY THIRD HAND IS ONE WAY OF MAKING IT LOOK LIKE THIRD HAND IS SIGNALING ENCOURAGEMENT, WHEN, IN FACT, HE IS NOT.
2. WHEN TRYING TO MASK WEAKNESS IN A SUIT (HEARTS), IT USUALLY PAYS TO DEVELOP A SIDE SUIT BEFORE DRAWING TRUMPS. IF YOU DRAW TRUMPS YOU RUN THE RISK OF A REVEALING DISCARD.

(47) SPOTS

East-West vulnerable
Dealer West

North
♠ 9 4 3 2
♡ A K Q 2
◇ 2
♣ A K 9 2

South
♠ A Q 7
♡ 10 4 3
◇ J 6
♣ Q J 8 7 6

West	North	East	South
1 ◇	Dbl.	Pass	3 ♣
3 ◇	5 ♣	Pass	Pass
Pass			

Opening lead: ◇ Q (Q from A K Q)

East plays the ◇ 3, count, and West continues with the ◇ A which you ruff with the ♣ 9, East following.

At trick three you cash the ♣ A, all following, and at trick four you lead a club to your queen, West shedding a diamond.

How do you continue?

SPOTS (Solution)

North
♠ 9 4 3 2
♡ A K Q 2
◇ 2
♣ A K 9 2

<table>
<tr><td>

West
♠ K J 8
♡ 9 8
◇ A K Q 10 9 8 7
♣ 5

</td><td>

East
♠ 10 6 5
♡ J 7 6 5
◇ 5 4 3
♣ 10 4 3

</td></tr>
</table>

South
♠ A Q 7
♡ 10 4 3
◇ J 6
♣ Q J 8 7 6

Cash the ♡ A K. If the ♡ J falls from West, cash the ♡ 10, enter dummy with a trump and discard a losing spade on a high heart. That's eleven tricks without the spade finesse.

If the ♡ J does not appear, cash the ♡ Q to see if hearts break 3-3. If they do, cash dummy's high trump and discard a spade on the long heart.

If East turns up with ♡ Jxxx, lead a low spade towards your hand. If East plays low, insert the ♠ 7, endplaying West. If East plays the ♠ 10 or ♠ J, cover with the ♠ Q once again endplaying West—if he has the ♠ 8. West will have to return a spade and you can play low from dummy.

Only if East plays the ♠ 8 are you in trouble. Big trouble. You can't make the hand if East started with 108x or J8x, so you must play East for 8xx and duck the trick. If West has the hoped for ♠ K J 10, he will have to win trick and will be endplayed.

KEY LESSON POINTERS

1. WHEN HOLDING AKQx FACING 10xx, ALLOW FOR THE POSSIBILITY OF Jx, AND TRY TO RETAIN A SIDE ENTRY TO THE HAND WITH THE AKQx.
2. SOMETIMES A STRIP AND END PLAY CAN BE EXECUTED WITHOUT DRAWING ALL OF THE TRUMPS. IF YOU CAN DUCK A TRICK INTO THE PLAYER WHO DOES NOT HAVE A SAFE TRUMP EXIT, HIS RETURN MAY COST HIS SIDE A TRICK.

(48) MAJOR TWO-SUITER

East-West vulnerable
Dealer East

North
♠ J 9 5
♡ J 10 7 5
♢ A 9 8 7 5
♣ 3

South
♠ A Q 10 8 7
♡ K Q 9 3 2
♢ 4
♣ K 2

East	South	West	North
1 ♣	1 ♠	2 ♣	2 ♠
3 ♣	3 ♡	Pass	4 ♡
Pass	Pass	Pass	

Opening lead: ♣ 4

East wins the ♣ A and shifts to the ♠ 3. What is your plan?

MAJOR TWO-SUITER (Solution)

North
♠ J 9 5
♡ J 10 7 5
◇ A 9 8 7 5
♣ 3

West
♠ K 6 4 2
♡ A 4
◇ 10 6 2
♣ 10 6 5 4

East
♠ 3
♡ 8 6
◇ K Q J 3
♣ A Q J 9 8 7

South
♠ A Q 10 8 7
♡ K Q 9 3 2
◇ 4
♣ K 2

No need to risk your contract by taking the spade finesse. Rise with the ♠ A, cash the ♣ K, discarding a spade, and drive out the ♡ A.

No matter how the adverse cards are divided you can lose no more than three tricks.

KEY LESSON POINTERS

1. DON'T PUT YOUR CONTRACT UP FOR GRABS WHEN YOU HAVE A GUARANTEED WAY TO INSURE IT.
2. DISCARDING A NON-LOSER FROM DUMMY ON A WINNER (IN ORDER TO SHORTEN DUMMY'S LENGTH) IS ONE WAY TO AVOID A RUFF.

(49) WHAT'S THE CATCH?

East-West vulnerable
Dealer South

North
♠ 5 4 3
♡ K
♢ A K J 10 8 7
♣ A 5 2

South
♠ K Q 6
♡ 10 6 5 3 2
♢ Q 2
♣ K 8 4

South	West	North	East
Pass	Pass	1 ♢	Pass
1 ♡	Pass	2 ♢	Pass
2 NT	Pass	3 NT	Pass
Pass	Pass		

Opening lead: ♠ J
East wins the ♠ A.

1. Which spade do you play if the lead of the jack denies a higher honor?
2. Which spade do you play if the lead of the jack does not deny a higher honor?

WHAT'S THE CATCH? (Solution)

North
♠ 5 4 3
♡ K
◇ A K J 10 8 7
♣ A 5 2

West
♠ J 10 9 8
♡ A J 9 7
◇ 5 4 3
♣ Q 6

East
♠ A 7 2
♡ Q 8 4
◇ 9 6
♣ J 10 9 7 3

South
♠ K Q 6
♡ 10 6 5 3 2
◇ Q 2
♣ K 8 4

1. The ♠ Q. You want to avoid a heart shift so you are making it easier for East to continue spades. Remember, East knows that you have both the king and queen of spades. If you play low at trick one, East might find the heart shift.

    The play of the ♠ Q sacrifices a trick, but it gives you a far better chance to land your contract—what the game is all about, after all.

2. The ♠ 6. East doesn't know whether West has led from the top of a sequence, or from a suit headed by the K J 10. Playing the ♠ 6 gives you the best chance of conning East into a spade continuation—exactly what you want.

KEY LESSON POINTERS

1. THE FIRST STEP IS TO KNOW YOUR OPPONENTS' LEAD CONVENTIONS.
2. THE SECOND STEP IS TO KNOW HOW TO USE THEM TO YOUR ADVANTAGE.
3. IF THEIR LEADS ARE AMBIGUOUS (J FROM AJ10, KJ10 or J109), TRY NOT TO PLAY A CARD THAT WILL CLARIFY THE AMBIGUITY. IF THEY WANT TO LIVE BY THE SWORD, LET THEM DIE BY THE SWORD.
4. WHEN YOU FEAR A SHIFT, FEIGN WEAKNESS IN THE SUIT THEY HAVE LED, EVEN AT THE COST OF AN OVERTRICK. IT ONLY HURTS FOR A LITTLE WHILE.

(50) STRAIGHTFORWARD BIDDING

Neither side vulnerable
Dealer West

North
♠ A J 3 2
♡ K Q 9 8 7
♢ K 2
♣ Q 7

South
♠ 9 8 7 5 4
♡ J 3 2
♢ A Q 7 6
♣ J

West	North	East	South
1 ♢	Dbl.	Pass	2 ♠
Pass	4 ♠	Pass	Pass
Pass			

Opening lead: ♡ A

West continues with the ♡ 6 which you win in your hand, East playing the ♡ 4 and then the ♡ 10.

You lead a low spade at trick three. West plays the ♠ Q which you win in dummy, East playing the ♠ 10.

How do you continue?

STRAIGHTFORWARD BIDDING (Solution)

North
♠ A J 3 2
♡ K Q 9 8 7
◇ K 2
♣ Q 7

West
♠ K Q 6
♡ A 6
◇ J 10 9 3
♣ A 10 5 3

East
♠ 10
♡ 10 5 4
◇ 8 5 4
♣ K 9 8 6 4 2

South
♠ 9 8 7 5 4
♡ J 3 2
◇ A Q 7 6
♣ J

It should be obvious that West has led from a doubleton heart and holds ♠ K Q 6. Furthermore, East is marked with a high club honor from West's failure to lead the ♣ K at trick one.

If you play a second spade, West will win and East will signal with a high club. West will lead a low club to East and get his heart ruff to defeat you one trick. What can you do about this?

Plenty. You can play four rounds of diamonds discarding two clubs from dummy. West will be on lead and will not be able to put East in with a club to get this heart ruff. You wind up losing one heart, one spade, and one diamond—but no club, and no heart ruff.

KEY LESSON POINTERS

1. TRANSFERRING AN ENTRY FROM ONE DEFENDER'S HAND TO AN-OTHER IS ONE WAY OF AVOIDING AN IMPENDING RUFF. IN THIS CASE EAST IS THE DANGER HAND BECAUSE HE CAN GIVE WEST A HEART RUFF. THEREFORE, YOU MUST CONCOCT A PLAN THAT WILL KEEP EAST OFF LEAD. PLAYING FOUR ROUNDS OF DIAMONDS, DISCARDING TWO CLUBS FROM DUMMY, SIMPLY TRANSFERS A CLUB LOSER INTO A DIAMOND LOSER, BUT IT DOES KEEP EAST OFF LEAD. YOU PLAY SO BRILLIANTLY.

APPENDIX (THEMES)

SECTION I (PLAY HANDS)

1. HOLD UP PLAY, PLAYING TO MAKE
2. DECEPTION, TRUMP REDUCTION
3. DECEPTION
4. THROW IN AND END PLAY
5. AVOIDING A RUFF
6. PLACING THE CARDS, CARD COMBINATIONS
7. PLACING THE CARDS, RETAINING CONTROL
8. AVOIDING A RUFF WITH A LOSER ON LOSER PLAY
9. AVOIDING AN IMPENDING RUFF, CARD COMBINATIONS
10. HANDLING A RUFF AND A SLUFF, TRUMP SAFETY PLAY
11. ELIMINATION PLAY
12. PLAYING FOR A SQUEEZE
13. UNBLOCKING
14. CREATING AN ENTRY TO AN ENTRYLESS DUMMY
15. AVOIDANCE
16. CARD COMBINATIONS
17. CARD COMBINATIONS, AVOIDING A RUFF
18. COAXING A DEFENSIVE ERROR
19. READING THE LEAD, STEALING EARLY, CARD COMBINATIONS
20. GUARDING AGAINST AN OVERRUFF
21. PLAYING THE ODDS
22. THREE-SUITED SQUEEZE
23. UNBLOCKING
24. AVOIDANCE
25. COAXING A DEFENSIVE ERROR EARLY. MAKING ASSUMPTIONS FROM THEIR BIDDING OR THEIR SILENCE

SECTION II (DEFENSIVE HANDS)

1. READING THE LEAD, UNBLOCKING, COUNTING PARTNER'S POINTS
2. KILLING A DUMMY ENTRY BY PLAYING SECOND HAND HIGH
3. COUNTING TRICKS, OVERCOMING A DECEPTIVE PLAY
4. FINDING THE WINNING DISCARD
5. UNBLOCKING, TRUMP PROMOTION
6. COUNTING TRICKS, CARD COMBINATIONS
7. TRUMP PROMOTION VIA A RUFF AND A SLUFF
8. GIVING PARTNER A LATER RUFF, GETTING A RUFF, UNBLOCKING
9. REFUSING TO RUFF, CARD COMBINATIONS
10. GIVING DECLARER A RUFF AND A SLUFF, END GAME VISUALIZATION
11. COUNTING THE HAND, SECOND HAND PLAY, CARD COMBINATIONS
12. AVOIDING A SQUEEZE
13. COUNTING, CASHING OUT EARLY
14. REFUSING A GREEK GIFT, ENTRY CONSIDERATIONS
15. OVERTAKING, ENTRY CONSIDERATIONS, GOING FOR A RUFF
16. SECOND HAND PLAY
17. SUIT PREFERENCE SIGNAL
18. COUNTING TRICKS, REFUSING TO COVER AN HONOR WITH AN HONOR
19. PROPER DISCARDING, PLAYING FOR THE ONLY CHANCE
20. VISUALIZING A TRUMP PROMOTION
21. READING PARTNER'S ATTITUDE SIGNAL
22. CARD COMBINATIONS, PLACING THE MISSING HONORS
23. COUNTING DECLARER'S TRICKS, READING A DISCARD
24. COUNTING DECLARER'S TRICKS, COUNTING THE HAND, LEADING THE PROPER CARD
25. COUNTING DECLARER'S TRICKS, CARD COMBINATIONS, ASSUMPTIONS

SECTION III (DEFENSIVE HANDS)

SECTION IV (PLAY HANDS)

Can't Find These Other Great Books on Improving your Bridge Play by Eddie Kantar ? Then Write Griffin Publishing.